# ECONOMICS

## THE REMARKABLE STORY OF
## HOW THE ECONOMY WORKS

BEN MATHEW

benmatheweconomics.com

Published by:
Run Rabbit Books
www.runrabbitbooks.com

ISBN-10: 0988669102
ISBN-13: 978-0988669109

# CONTENTS

PART 1


THE MAIN STORY

# CHAPTER 1

# What is an Economy?

Economics is the study of the economy. So we first need to figure out what an economy is. The global economy teeming with seven billion people is too big to wrap our minds around. So we'll start with a smaller one.

A middle-aged accountant named Max goes on a vacation cruise, has one too many free drinks, falls overboard, grabs a passing log, drifts for days, and washes up on the sandy beaches of a pleasant-looking island. He lies there for a while, hoping the kindly native islanders will carry him to their hut and feed him coconuts and spring water. When no one shows up all afternoon, he realizes he's alone. He sits up and takes stock of his situation.

Max wants some things. He wants food, clothes, shelter, entertainment, good health, companionship, and to not be eaten by a tiger. How can he get these things?

He has some resources at his disposal. The island has coconut trees, farmable land, forests, wild turkeys, and streams filled with trout. We call these resources *capital*. Max also has the ability to work. He can perform physical tasks like lifting a rock and climbing a tree. He can perform mental tasks like figuring out which coconut tree has more coconuts. This ability to work—to perform physical tasks with his body and mental tasks with his brain—we call *labor*.

Max needs to use what he has (coconut trees, streams, wild turkeys, a strong back, and a sharp mind) to get what he wants (log cabin, shirts, coconuts, and spring water). He clears land and plants pineapples, climbs coconut trees to collect coconuts, weaves a shirt out of tall grass, and cuts down trees to build a cabin. He befriends a dog for company, and dances around a bonfire for entertainment.

These activities constitute Max's economy. Max *produces* what he wants using the labor and capital available to him, and he *consumes* it to satisfy his wants. This daily rhythm of producing and consuming constitutes his economy. The economy, broadly defined, is his daily life.

Now, instead of just Max on a small island, let us put seven billion people together on a much bigger island called Earth, and we have the global economy. The scale is bigger, but many of the problems are the same. Like Max, these seven billion people want food, clothes, shelter, companionship, and entertainment. Like Max, they have to figure out a way to get these things using the limited resources that they have on their planet. They harness their land, minerals, forests, and sunlight to produce cornflakes, aspirin, TV shows, and townhouses, which they then consume. Whether as cooks or carpenters, bankers or yoga instructors, shoppers or moviegoers, students or retirees, this describes what everyone does all day. Every morning, seven billion people wake up and play their part in an incredibly vast and intricate ballet of production and consumption that constitutes the global economy, and life itself.

# CHAPTER 2

# A Good Economy

An economy works well if it makes good use of its limited resources to satisfy people's desires as best as possible. It works badly if it wastes resources, builds the wrong things using the wrong techniques, and gets them to the wrong people.

Max has limited time and resources on his hands. If he spends all day building a massive log cabin, he will go hungry. If he spends all day collecting coconuts, he will be cold at night. If he spends all day collecting coconuts and building his cabin, he can't dance around a bonfire. Sure, he would like more of everything—a supersize cabin, plenty of coconuts, and bonfire dancing day and night. But he can't have that. He has to make do with the limited time and resources that he has available to him, and he has to use them wisely to make sure that what he's doing lines up with what he really wants.

Like Max on his island, we need to make sure that we, here on Planet Earth, are doing the right things with our limited resources. In 2010, the world used its limited resources to produce 58,478,810 cars and 1,011 airliners. Was this the right thing to do? Should we instead have produced fewer cars and more airliners? Maybe you got a job closer to where you live, so you can now walk to work. So the world does not need as many cars. And your daughter just moved clear across the country and you plan to fly there often to see her. So the world needs more airliners. Did you send a note describing the changes in your life to whoever's in charge of building cars and airliners? If you didn't, how would they know to build fewer cars and more airliners to accommodate you? How can they figure out how many cars and airliners to build if nobody is sending them this information? Max has it easy. He is the only one on the island, and it is easy for him to know what he wants and what he can do. But for us here on Planet Earth with seven billion people, each with our own complicated life, we could get this terribly wrong.

And terribly wrong we get it. The world economy as a whole is a badly-run operation. Let me grade economies on a scale of zero to ten. A grade of zero means total dysfunction: everyone in the economy is starving because all they do is dig holes and fill them back up. A grade of ten means perfection: everything is done exactly right. The worst-run parts of the global economy are places like Somalia where famines still kill people. I give Somalia a two. India works a little better and gets a three. China gets a four. France gets a five. And the best-run major economy in the world, the United States, gets only a six. In other words, the best-run economies in the world are somewhat dysfunction-al, and the worst-run economies are very dysfunctional.

If you live in the United States, improving the economy from a somewhat dysfunctional six to a well-functioning nine would greatly improve your life. It would be like living in a supereconomy, the likes of which the world has never seen. You would find it easier to get jobs, be able to work fewer hours, live a longer and healthier life, not die waiting for a kidney transplant, find cheaper and better housing more easily, live closer to work, zip along highways without being stuck in traffic, go on more vacations, have more money socked away for retirement, and send your kids to better schools. Cancer might have been cured.

If all this sounds fanciful, imagine you've lived your whole life in Zimbabwe, where people live on $3 a day and usually die before their fiftieth birthday. Somebody tells you about this wonderful place—this land of plenty—where ordinary people live in two-thousand-square-foot mansions, own two cars, eat all the cake they want, fly in airplanes, and live to eighty! If TV didn't bring you a glimpse of life in the Western world, you wouldn't believe it. That's the stark differ-ence between a seriously dysfunctional two and a somewhat dysfunctional six. Advancing from a somewhat dysfunctional six to a well-functioning nine would not be a whole lot less spectacular. We just don't understand what we're missing because there is no well-functioning economy to serve as an example. We must imagine it.

How can we get our economies to work better? There are two things we need. First, the *rule of law*. Nobody is going to plant cabbages if roving bands of thugs or corrupt policemen are going to take their cabbages away at harvest time. Second, we need *good laws*. Nobody is going to plant cabbages if the law requires them to dump their harvest in the swamp or give it all to the taxman.

Countries in Africa, Asia, Eastern Europe, Latin America, and the Middle East struggle with the rule of law. Weak and corrupt government is the norm in these places. I grew up in India and experienced it firsthand. A water department official once shut off our water supply because we didn't know we were supposed to "tip" him when he came by to ostensibly check if everything was okay. People foolish enough to go to court to settle a dispute face decades of an interminable judicial process that involves both parties bribing the judge. Truck drivers cannot go far without being shaken down by the police. Corruption is so ingrained that when a famously incorrupt senior police official was newly posted to our town, our neighbor worried about how she could get anything done without bribes. This neighbor was no gangster. She was a schoolteacher. She just couldn't imagine a public official doing anything—legal or illegal—without a bribe.

Only a thin slice of the world has escaped such lawlessness. These are the fortunate few living in Western Europe, the United States, Canada, Australia, New Zealand, and Japan. Sure, there is corruption in these places too. But it is not nearly as routine, pervasive, intrusive, and stifling as in the rest of the world. The government, however imperfect, discharges its basic duty of maintaining law and order reasonably well. People can plant cabbages without worrying about gangsters showing up. They can water their cabbages without city officials shutting off their water supply to extract bribes. They can truck their cabbages across town without being shaken down by the police. This is a big part of why these economies work better than others.

How can we strengthen the rule of law in lawless lands? I'm afraid I don't have the answer to that. My expertise as an economist lies in the second half of the equation: if we have a society that is more or less governed by laws, what kind of laws should we have? Here, the whole world comes up short. The West does have better laws than most of the rest of the world. But even the best have lots of bad laws that clog their economies and prevent them from working nearly as well as they could.

Unlike a corrupt political infrastructure—which most people recognize as a bad thing but are powerless against—bad laws exist mostly because people think they are good laws. And they think that way because they don't know enough economics to understand the consequences of those laws. Special interest groups—everyone from farmers and physicians to car manufacturers and internet retailers—take advantage of this ignorance and push through laws that further their own interests at the expense of everyone else.

The laws you see today are a direct consequence of economic illiteracy in the general population. If every voter learned economics tonight, the laws would change tomorrow. If that happened, you would start experiencing some of the benefits within a few months. Other benefits would take longer to surface as the economy slowly adjusted to the new rules. But within five years, your life would be a lot better. Within fifteen years, the economy would have pretty much fully responded to the new laws. You would then be living in a supereconomy.

# CHAPTER 3

# Efficient Is Good

An economy contains many people with competing desires. This naturally implies much disagreement about what needs to be done. Sammy wants a bigger house and Jimmy wants more pancakes. Since the economy's resources are limited, if Sammy gets a bigger house, Jimmy can't have more pancakes. Who should the economy satisfy: Sammy or Jimmy? This is the question of *distribution*. How should the output of the economy—the fruits of its labor and capital—be divided up between people?

Right now, we divide it up pretty unevenly. A banker in Manhattan might get thousands of times what a construction worker in Nairobi gets. Maybe you think that's okay, maybe you don't. For those of you who are interested in this issue, I will discuss later what we can do to make things more equitable. But for now, let's put aside the difficult issue of distribution and focus instead on something just as important but refreshingly straightforward and uncontroversial.

Let's go back to Max. There are no distributional issues in Max's economy because Max is the only one around. All of the island's output should clearly go to him. Max's economy needs only to make sure that the limited resources on the island are used judiciously to best satisfy Max's desires. For example, Max shouldn't build an oversize cabin while going hungry. That's a bad use of his time because he would rather have a full stomach than an oversize cabin. If, in spite of this, he foolishly builds an oversize cabin while going hungry, we say that Max's economy is being *inefficient*. Inefficient simply means that the situation can be unambiguously improved upon. Something is wrong, and fixing it will improve someone's life without hurting anyone else. So inefficient means that a mistake was made. A well-run economy cannot be inefficient because it cannot make mistakes.

Let's look at another example, this one involving two people. There's an almond and a cashew. Jane prefers the almond and Jillian prefers the cashew. But Jillian eats the almond and Jane eats the cashew. A clear mistake, right? The economy messed up. If, instead, Jillian had eaten the cashew and Jane had eaten the almond, both of them would have been better off. This is not a matter of distribution—about who should have more and who should have less. This is not a matter of making one person better off at the expense of another. Something was broken, and fixing it would have helped both parties without hurting anyone else.

When I say that the economy is not working well, I mean that it contains inefficiencies like these—

opportunities for improvement. The real errors of the real economy may not be quite as obvious as in the simplified scenarios I just made up. The world is a big and complicated place, and mistakes hide in the complexity. But a trained eye can find them. They are everywhere, and they are every bit as absurd as my made-up examples. I'll show you three of these errors. They are not necessarily the most egregious errors— just three examples to illustrate the problem.

## The Apartment Swap

You have lived in the same apartment in Upper Manhattan for many years. Because of rent control laws that limit how much your rent can rise each year, you are now paying only $1,000 per month. If you move out, your landlord can rent it out to someone else for twice as much. I am in the same situation, except my apartment is in Lower Manhattan. I too am paying only $1,000 per month for an apartment that will fetch twice as much in the open market. Because of job changes, I would like to move into your apartment in Upper Manhattan and you would like to move into my apartment in Lower Manhattan. But if we switch apartments, both of us would have to pay more in rent. So we decide to stay put and face a tedious commute, every day, in opposite directions.

The economy malfunctioned. It placed us in the wrong apartments. If we had switched apartments, both of us would have been better off and no one else worse off. But the rules of the game prevented that from happening. Our economy didn't have a system in place to put us in the right apartments. It was inefficient.

## The Fast Lane

Your mother-in-law calls from the hospital to say that your wife is going to deliver the baby sooner than expected. Eager to be present at the birth of your child, you drop everything, rush to your car, and get on the freeway. Soon, you hit traffic. It's stop and go as far as you can see. You're not going to make it. You seethe, swear, and lean on your horn.

You look out your window and see my wife and me breezing by on our way to the mall. We are on the High Occupancy Vehicle (HOV) lane—the fast lane where only vehicles carrying two or more people are allowed. We're in no particular hurry, but we get to go on the fast lane because there are two of us in the car. You're in a big hurry, but you're not allowed on because there is only one of you in the car. Those are the rules.

The rules created an inefficiency. You would have been willing to pay hundreds of dollars for the privilege of driving on the fast lane to get to the hospital on time. We, on the other hand, value getting to the mall quickly at only a couple of dollars. If the economy took

$10 from you and put you in the fast lane, and gave that money to my wife and me and put us in the regular lane, all three of us would have been better off and no one else worse off. But the economy didn't do it. It malfunctioned. It did not have a system in place to ensure that you were on the fast lane instead of us. It was inefficient.

## (IN)FLEXIBLE SPENDING ACCOUNTS

The United States has a program called the Flexible Spending Account (the "flex account"). Money you put into this account is not taxed, but you can use it only for medical and childcare expenses. The tax savings are attractive, so a lot of people sign up. The catch is that you have to decide before the start of the year how much money you will put into the account for that year. If you put in too much and don't use it all up before the end of the year, you lose the unused money—ouch! If you put in too little and run out before the end of the year, you can't use tax-free money for the rest of your medical and childcare expenses that year—also ouch! So you have to guess your future expenses as best as you can, fill up your account accordingly, and hope you didn't put in too much or too little.

The problem with this arrangement is that people who have money left over in their flex accounts toward the end of the year will start spending that money on things they don't need just to use up their flex money. They'll stockpile cough syrup on the slim chance that they'll need it before it expires. Meanwhile, people who have a cough, but no flex money left, might forgo the cough syrup.

This creates inefficiencies. Say a bottle of cough syrup costs $5. Lara has a cough, but no flex money left. So she'll have to pay for the cough syrup out of her pocket. She values the cough syrup at only $3, so she doesn't buy it. Boris isn't sick, but has a lot of flex money left. Though he values the cough syrup at just $0.10, he still buys a bottle to use up his flex money.

This was inefficient. If the economy took the cough syrup from Boris and gave it to Lara, and took $2 from Lara and gave it to Boris, both Lara and Boris would have been better off and no one else worse off. The situation could have been unambiguously improved. The economy messed up. It didn't get the cough syrup to the right person. It was inefficient.

I could go on, but I'll stop here. These examples should be enough to give you a sense of what inefficiencies are and how prevalent they are. They tell us that our economy is not working properly, and that we could be doing better.

# CHAPTER 4

# Central Planning

It's showtime! We're going to build a supereconomy that gets everything exactly right. Remember, there are two things we need: the rule of law, and good laws. Assume we already have a law-abiding society in place. All we need to do is put in the right kind of laws to get the economy humming.

A body of rules arising from a coherent set of principles can be called a system. There are two big systems around: central planning and free markets. No economy is fully one or the other. All real-world economies are a mishmash of both, plus some random laws thrown in. But we can usefully place economies on a spectrum between pure central planning and pure free markets. The Soviet Union leaned toward central planning; Western Europe and the United States were more free market. We will try out central planning in this chapter and free markets in the next.

The idea behind central planning is straightforward: appoint someone to decide what the economy should do and how it should be done. Of course, our economy is so big and complicated that one person cannot possibly figure it all out. So we end up appointing a large team—a big planning department with lots of different divisions and subdivisions that are responsible for different parts of the economy. These planners will decide how to use all of the labor and capital in the economy, and they will decide who gets the resulting output. They will calculate whether to build a boat or a jet ski, whether to use aluminum or steel to build it, whether you or I will work on it, and whether you or I will ride it. Once they make their master plan, all the people follow the blueprint and produce what they are supposed to produce and consume what they are supposed to consume.

Though many centrally planned economies are politically autocratic, they don't have to be. Before changing course in the early 1990s, India did a lot of central planning while remaining a democracy. In centrally planned economies that are democracies, the planning board serves at the pleasure of the voters. If the government does not do a good job of planning and administering the economy, voters can always vote it out, install a new government, and hope for better.

The great attraction of central planning is complete flexibility in distribution. Outcomes can be made as equal as we like. Everyone gets a fair share of three loaves of bread a week. Everyone works a fair share of forty hours a week. No one is born with a silver spoon in their mouth. No one will be homeless and hungry. Socialism—the great movement that instituted central planning in half the world—had as its rallying cry, "From each according to his ability, to each according to his need." Now isn't that an attractive proposition when you see the idle landowner take home more of the harvest than the field hand who ploughed from sunrise to sunset?

But the system has its flaws, and the flaws are fatal. We did not know this back in 1900. Back then, many economists thought that central planning was a great idea. But then we had a worldwide experiment that played out over the course of the twentieth century. By 1950, half the world had adopted central planning while the other half remained free market. The result of the experiment was decisive. Every economy that adopted central planning did badly. The more they relied on central planning, the worse they did. By 1980, centrally planned economies were in serious crisis. There was no bread on the shelves, no produce in the bins. Farms were covered with weeds, and walls were covered with peeling paint. Electricity came and went. People risked their lives trying to flee their failing economies. Slowly these countries realized that their economic system wasn't working. One by one, in fits and starts, they began to dismantle central planning and adopt free markets.

What happened? What went wrong? Two things: it's hard to plan, and it's hard to make people follow the plan. Think about how hard it is to make a good master plan for the entire economy. The world is so fantastically big and complicated. There are literally trillions of pieces of information needed to make that plan. Could the planning department really keep tabs on your life well enough to know that you would like to go on a diet and so they should make less chocolate ice cream and more nonfat yogurt? Can you think of any organization—whether a government agency or a nonprofit or a corporation—that could, with any budget, pull off such a feat? Executives at large corporations like GE and Walmart struggle to manage the labor and capital that they direct. A planning department would have to plan an operation bigger than tens of thousands of GEs and Walmarts combined. It's just impossible.

Hang on, you say. Let's not have one giant planning department in charge of the world economy or even a country's economy. How about planning at a smaller scale like a city or an industry: little planning departments, each in charge of its own little turf? Good try, but that won't work either because different parts of the economy are interconnected. We consume such diverse and complex products—breakfast cereal, jet engines, and hip surgeries—that no one person, or city, or even country, can produce it all. We are forced to specialize in a few little things and then trade with others for most of what we need. So we end up having to coordinate across far-flung corners of the globe.

That means we can't plan for Kansas without thinking about Thailand. In 2011, heavy rains caused flooding in Thailand. Many hard drive manufacturers had factories there, and production was disrupted. This meant that people in Kansas should conserve their hard disk space: take fewer photos and don't back them up as frequently. So Kansas planners have to get on the phone with Thailand planners. And we are back to square one—the complexity is again overwhelming and unmanageable.

The enormity of the task is illustrated in a powerful essay called "I, Pencil" that came out in 1958. It describes how making even an ordinary wooden pencil requires mindboggling feats of cooperation and coordination by millions of people in the economy, not one of whom actually knows how to make a pencil. Most of them are not even aware that they are involved in making a pencil. The essay captures the sheer scale of the specialization, interdependence, and coordination required to run even a tiny portion of the economy. I reproduce the relevant parts here:

### I, Pencil
#### Leonard Read

I am a lead pencil—the ordinary wooden pencil familiar to all boys and girls and adults who can read and write.

Writing is both my vocation and my avocation; that's all I do.

You may wonder why I should write a genealogy. Well, to begin with, my story is interesting. And, next, I am a mystery—more so than a tree or a sunset or even a flash of lightning. But, sadly, I am taken for granted by those who use me, as if I were a mere incident and without background. This supercilious attitude relegates me to the level of the commonplace.

I, Pencil, simple though I appear to be, merit your wonder and awe, a claim I shall attempt to prove. [...] I have a profound lesson to teach. And I can teach this lesson better than can an automobile or an airplane or a mechanical dishwasher because—well, because I am seemingly so simple.

Simple? Yet, not a single person on the face of this earth knows how to make me. This sounds fantastic, doesn't it? Especially when it is realized that there are about one and one-half billion of my kind produced in the U.S.A. each year.

Pick me up and look me over. What do you see? Not much meets the eye—there's some wood, lacquer, the printed labeling, graphite lead, a bit of metal, and an eraser.

Just as you cannot trace your family tree back very far, so is it impossible for me to name and explain all my antecedents. But I would like to suggest enough of them to impress upon you the richness and complexity of my background.

My family tree begins with what in fact is a tree, a cedar of straight grain that grows in Northern California and Oregon. Now contemplate all the saws and trucks and rope and the countless other gear used in harvesting and carting the cedar logs to the railroad siding. Think of all the persons and the numberless skills that went into their fabrication: the mining of ore, the making of steel and its refinement into saws, axes, motors; the growing of hemp and bringing it through all the stages to heavy and strong rope; the logging camps with their beds and mess halls, the cookery and the raising of all the foods. Why, untold thousands of persons had a hand in every cup of coffee the loggers drink!

The logs are shipped to a mill in San Leandro, California. Can you imagine the individuals who make flat cars and rails and railroad engines and who construct and install the communication systems incidental thereto? These legions are among my antecedents.

Consider the millwork in San Leandro. The cedar logs are cut into small, pencil-length slats less than one-fourth of an inch in thickness. These are kiln-dried and then tinted for the same reason women put rouge on their faces. People prefer that I look pretty, not a pallid white. The slats are waxed and kiln-dried again. How many skills went into the making of the tint and the kilns, into supplying the heat, the light and power, the belts, motors, and all the other things a mill requires?

Sweepers in the mill among my ancestors? Yes, and included are the men who poured the concrete for the dam of a Pacific Gas & Electric Company hydroplant which supplies the mill's power!

Don't overlook the ancestors present and distant who have a hand in transporting sixty carloads of slats across the nation from California to Wilkes-Barre!

Once in the pencil factory—$4,000,000 in machinery and building, all capital accumulated by thrifty and saving parents of mine—each slat is given eight grooves by a complex machine, after which another machine lays leads in every other slat, applies glue, and places another slat atop—a lead sandwich, so to speak. Seven brothers and I are mechanically carved from this "wood-clinched" sandwich.

My "lead" itself—it contains no lead at all—is complex. The graphite is mined in Ceylon. Consider these miners and those who make their many tools and the makers of the paper sacks in which the graphite is shipped and those who make the string that ties the sacks and those who put them aboard ships and those who make the ships. Even the lighthouse keepers along the way assisted in my birth—and the harbor pilots.

The graphite is mixed with clay from Mississippi in which ammonium hydroxide is used in the refining process. Then wetting agents are added such as sulfonated tallow—animal fats chemically reacted with sulfuric acid. After passing through numerous machines, the mixture finally appears as endless extrusions—as from a sausage grinder—cut to size, dried, and baked for several hours at 1,850 degrees Fahrenheit. To increase their strength and smoothness the leads are then treated with a hot mixture which includes candelilla wax from Mexico, paraffin wax, and hydrogenated natural fats.

My cedar receives six coats of lacquer. Do you know all of the ingredients of lacquer? Who would think that the growers of castor beans and the refiners of castor oil are a part of it? They are. Why, even the processes by which the lacquer is made a beautiful yellow involves the skills of more persons than one can enumerate!

Observe the labeling. That's a film formed by applying heat to carbon black mixed with resins. How do you make resins and what, pray, is carbon black?

My bit of metal—the ferrule—is brass. Think of all the persons who mine zinc and copper and those who have the skills to make shiny sheet brass from these products of nature. Those black rings on my ferrule are black nickel. What is black nickel and how is it applied? The complete story of why the center of my ferrule has no black nickel on it would take pages to explain.

Then there's my crowning glory, inelegantly referred to in the trade as "the plug," the part man uses to erase the errors he makes with me. An ingredient called "factice" is what does the erasing. It is a rubber-like product made by reacting rape seed oil from the Dutch East Indies with sulfur chloride. Rubber, contrary to the common notion, is only for binding purposes. Then, too, there are numerous vulcanizing and accelerating agents. The pumice comes from Italy; and the pigment which gives "the plug" its color is cadmium sulfide.

Does anyone wish to challenge my earlier assertion that no single person on the face of this earth knows how to make me?

Actually, millions of human beings have had a hand in my creation, no one of whom even knows more than a very few of the others. Now, you may say that I go too far in relating the picker of a coffee berry in far off Brazil and food growers elsewhere to my creation; that this is an extreme position. I shall stand by my claim. There isn't a single person in all these millions, including the president of the pencil company, who contributes more than a tiny, infinitesimal bit of know-how. [...]

Whew! Boggles the mind, doesn't it? No wonder central planners struggle to do their job.

But let's put this problem aside for now. Suppose that, by some miracle, the planning department comes through with the perfect master plan. What then? The battle is still not won. People now have to follow the plan. If the plan says you should knead the dough, then you should knead the dough. But you don't like to knead the dough. Why would you knead the dough if you get your three loaves of bread anyway? So you surf the web instead. But won't your supervisor force you to knead the dough? Not at all—your supervisor gets his three loaves of bread whether he does the unpleasant task of supervising you or slacks off himself. So he's on the internet too, forwarding you funny videos about cats flushing toilets. So now everyone is watching cat videos on YouTube, and no one is kneading the dough.

Even if the grand master plan is perfect, without a system of incentives to execute it, it is worthless. You have to find a way to reward people for doing the right thing and punish them for doing the wrong thing. Accomplishing that is harder than it seems. Companies struggle to get everyone from the intern to the CEO to act in the best interest of the company. Imagine trying to do that for the entire population. Creating the right incentives and monitoring performance are subtle, complex, and altogether difficult tasks. Planned economies simply do not get them right. Central planning failed because the master plan is too hard to make and too hard to execute.

## CHAPTER 5

# Free Markets

If central planning does not work, what else can we try? An alternative—one that much of the world is moving toward—is the free market system, also known as capitalism. It solves many of the defects of central planning in a neat and elegant way. It does have some problems, which we will get to. But almost all economists today—left, right, and center—agree that the free market system works better than central planning. Disagreements remain about how to fix specific defects of the free market system, but not about whether to adopt the system. Nobel Prize-winning economist Robert Solow of M.I.T., a steadfast liberal who advised the Kennedy administration, writes:

> Everyone has known for a long time that a complicated industrial economy is either a market economy or a mess. The real issues are pragmatic. Which of the defects of a "free," unregulated economy should be repaired by regulation, subsidization, or taxation? Which of them may have to be tolerated (and perhaps compensated), at least in part, because the best available fix would have even more costly side-effects? [*The New Republic*, November 16, 2012]

Most economists, regardless of where they fall on the political spectrum, will agree with this assessment. That's a remarkable consensus cutting across diverse values and politics: the free market system works better than central planning. So what is this system, and how does it work?

The free market system is in many ways the polar opposite of central planning. Central planning takes a top-down approach: install an economy-wide CEO to decide what to do. The free market system takes a bottom-up, grassroots approach: delegate all decision-making to the masses and let them figure it out on their own. It relies on billions of decisions made every day by every person in the economy. Should I grab that coffee on my way to work? Should I work as a teacher or a carpenter? Should I buy an iPhone or an Android? Should I invest in Toyota or Starbucks? It's a wholesale delegation of decision-making power to us ordinary people. In a centrally planned economy, we decide nothing. In a market economy, we decide everything.

Setting up the free market system is simple. First, we hand over all of the resources in the economy—all labor and capital—to the people living in the economy. We can give everyone an equal share if we like. Or we can give more to one and less to the other. The person to whom we give a particular resource is said to *own* that resource. The owner of a resource can do whatever he or she wants with it.

Okay, so let's do this. Let's divide up the capital first. It's pretty arbitrary—the land over here goes to Matt, the river over there goes to Mary, and those yonder coconut trees go to Marty. Done. Now, on to labor. In principle, we can hand out labor any way we want. We can give Matt's labor to Mary, and Mary's labor to Marty. But one person's labor being owned by another is slavery, and we don't want that. So we're going to give Matt's labor to Matt, Mary's labor to Mary, and Marty's labor to Marty. Done.

Now all we need to do is let people make whatever deals they want to make with each other. So, for example, Matt and Mary can make the following deal: *Matt shall give Mary an acre of land and Mary shall give Matt fifty gallons of water from her river.* We won't waste our time pondering the whys and wherefores of any deal. All we'll do is enforce the contracts. So if Mary takes the land but does not give the water, Matt can go to court to force Mary to keep her end of the deal. So the government plans nothing. It just enforces the deals that people make with each other.

That's it. We're done. We have handed over all labor and capital to individuals, and we'll be enforcing their deals. This is a piece of cake for the government compared to central planning. But the googabazillion dollar question is: will it work? The enormous task of running the economy—planning and deciding and coordinating—still has to be done. We've just shifted all of the work from the government to ordinary people. Will it work?

It's not at all obvious that this will work. Remember, the economy is unimaginably complicated. Every person will need to coordinate with billions of other people on the planet to get it right. Central planners couldn't handle the complexity. Can people, left to their own devices in a free market system, do any better?

It turns out that they can. It's astonishing, but every day, the free market system coordinates billions of people across the world in an unimaginably vast and intricate ballet of epic proportions. But how? Does a ballet not need a director? Does an army not need a general? Does an orchestra not need a conductor? How can individuals in an economy not need a commander-in-chief of some sort to coordinate their actions? How does the crowd end up performing a symphony instead of devolving into cacophony and chaos?

A Scottish philosopher by the name of Adam Smith figured out the answer and wrote it down in a book called *An Inquiry into the Nature and Causes of the Wealth of Nations*. The massive tome was published in 1776 and invented modern economics. All economists have a copy on their shelf, and some have even read parts of it.

# CHAPTER 6

# Wheeling and Dealing

So what did Adam Smith say? How does the magic happen? How do individuals in a free market economy coordinate without a commander-in-chief telling them what to do? How does the orchestra play a symphony without a conductor? The next four chapters tell the story.

The secret lies in the deals that people make with each other. These deals—or trades—are the interfaces through which every person communicates and coordinates with the rest of society. That's how people figure out what note to play and when. Our attempts to trade with the people around us force us to take stock of the larger economy and act correctly in the larger context. We don't explicitly think about the larger context when we pursue our deals. But, indirectly, without our knowing it, we are syncing with the rest of society.

Let's look at a day in the life of you—a person living in a free market economy. You wake up in the morning with the labor and capital that you own. Your labor is your ability to perform mental and physical tasks over the course of the day. You are good at making spreadsheets and installing kitchen cabinets, can concentrate for eight hours a day, and can lift two hundred pounds. You also own the following assets: a house, a car, $7,000 in your bank account, and $40,000 in stocks and bonds. This is your capital. What you're going to do today is trade this labor and capital that you have for the things that you want. You accomplish this by participating in a variety of deals over the course of the day. Some of these deals will be struck today, others would have been struck a few days or months or years ago.

Let's first look at what you do with your labor. You are going to spend eight hours at your job designing cars for Ford Motor Company. That means that you decided to let the owners of Ford use your labor today in exchange for the $200 that they will pay you for the day's work. You had other options as well. You could have instead done accounting for Toyota ($300), or flipped burgers for McDonald's ($60), or painted a sunset ($12), or replaced your kitchen faucet ($80 saved by not having to hire a plumber), or just watched TV ($0). But you decided that designing cars for Ford was the most attractive of all of these deals. The other options either paid less (burger flipping) or were less fun (accounting).

Now on to your capital. You live in the main floor of your house, so you're not going to trade that part of your capital with anyone else. But you rent your basement to a graduate student who attends a nearby university. So you traded that part of your capital for $800 per month in rent. Again, you considered all competing offers, including a rock band that needed a place to record their album and a family with rambunctious kids. But you decided that the trade with the graduate student was the most attractive deal for you.

As for your car, you're going to keep that for your own use. So no trade there.

What about the $7,000 in the bank? Are you going to let someone else use that money today? It's called lending. You hand over your money to someone for the day (or week or year), and they pay you interest in return. Just like you get rent for renting out your basement, you get interest for renting out your money. But you decide not to lend that money to your nephew who wants to build a social network for pets. You leave it in the bank. The interesting thing about banks is that they lend that money out for you whether or not you explicitly ask them to. That's why they are able to provide you with free ATM services and sometimes pay a modest interest. So it turns out that you will be lending that money to someone today after all—maybe even to your nephew, if he went and got a loan from your bank after you turned him down!

Finally, what are you doing with the $40,000 that you have invested in stocks and bonds? Buying Google bonds is the same as lending money to Google. Buying

Google stock is almost the same as lending money to Google, except that you don't know ahead of time how much interest they'll pay you. (They'll pay you a lot if the company does well, and little or none if the company does badly.)

So by using your money to buy stocks and bonds and placing the rest in a bank account, you have effectively lent out all of your money today to other people for interest. You have now rented out most of your capital—everything except the car and the main floor of the house is being used by someone else today. You are quite the wheeler and dealer, aren't you? Quite the capitalist!

So you have now rented out most of your labor and capital to others for the day. In return, you have collected $200 as wages for your labor, $26 as rent for your basement, $1 as interest and fee waivers for the money in your bank account, $2.25 as interest for the money you invested in bonds, and $3.75 as interest for the money you invested in stocks. That makes for a total haul of $233 today.

These dollar bills are not ends in and of themselves. You can't eat them, wear them or get entertained by them. They are just tokens that you will now proceed to exchange for the things that you really want: a cup of coffee, clothes, groceries, music downloads, movie tickets, and a new kitchen faucet. This is you in the role of consumer now. You are surrounded by a dizzying array of deals that the rest of society stands ready to make with you. Black coffee ($1.95) or café mocha ($3.50)? Movie at the theater ($9.95) or rent a DVD ($3.95)? Ranch house in the suburbs ($350,000) or condo downtown ($575,000)? A pound of broccoli ($0.99) or a pound of zucchini ($1.25)? Socks with zebra stripes ($1.99) or socks with pink polka dots ($2.99)? You get to decide which of these trades you're going to make with the people around you. You got $233 selling your labor and capital for the day and you will now use it to get the things that you want.

You may have noted a cycle here. Every day, you rent out your labor and capital to get dollars, and then you use those same dollars to obtain a portion of the economy's output. The first half of the cycle puts you in the role of producer, where your labor and capital are harnessed to produce output. The second half puts you in the role of consumer, where you get to enjoy a share of that output. You can hear the echo of Max's daily rhythm of producing and consuming—only yours is part of a larger and more complex process. Your labor and capital were used to produce the economy's output, and you got to consume some of that output. In the free market system, the way in which this got done involved your constantly trading with others, both in your role as producer and as consumer. You wheeled and dealed your way through a day of production and consumption.

CHAPTER 7

# The Price Is Right

So everyone is wheeling and dealing in the free market economy. But does all of this wheeling and dealing and personal decision-making lead to a well-running economy or an economy riddled with inefficiencies? Is the outcome going to be symphony or chaos?

It seems unlikely that this will work. When you think about whether to work at Ford or Toyota, you're not thinking about what's best for the economy—you're only thinking about what's best for you. But what's best for you may not be what's best for the economy. Maybe your not going to Toyota snarled their production line and destroyed thousands of cars. Maybe the band that wanted to rent your basement was Pink Floyd, and now they can't record *Wish You Were Here*. Maybe you should have gotten zucchini instead of broccoli because you like them the same and there's not much broccoli left. So we lost thousands of cars, everyone's listening to 'N Sync, and we've run out of broccoli—because you thought only about you and not about the wider economy.

But fear not. Astonishingly, you did do all the right things. You were right to spend the day designing cars for Ford (and not balancing books for Toyota). You were right to rent your basement to the graduate student (and not to Pink Floyd). You were right to eat broccoli (and not zucchini). All of your choices were efficient. Isn't that astonishing? How in the world did you end up doing all the right things when you weren't even trying? It's like you painted the *Mona Lisa* in your sleep.

Here's what happened. When you decided which job to take and who to rent your basement to and what groceries to buy, yes, you were thinking only about yourself. But, unwittingly, you also acted correctly in the context of society as a whole because of one little thing: the price at which people offered you your trades. In a perfectly free market economy—free from interference by taxes, subsidies, monopolies, cartels, and other such distortions—that price will indeed be right. It will be right in the sense that it will get you to do the right thing. The price will guide you to that one efficient choice lurking amongst a thousand inefficient ones.

Let's look at your decision to eat broccoli instead of zucchini for dinner. That decision was influenced by the fact that broccoli was $0.99 per pound and zucchini was $1.25 per pound. If broccoli had been sufficiently more expensive and zucchini had been sufficiently cheaper, you would have eaten zucchini instead. The prices were guiding you.

But were they guiding you correctly? It'll take me two more chapters to prove that, yes, prices get us to make the right choices. But, in the meantime, to show that prices at least push us in the right direction, let's see what happened behind the scenes when you were making your decisions.

Suppose broccoli suddenly becomes scarce because of a bad harvest. What will happen to the price of broccoli? It will shoot up, right? That higher price will then persuade you to switch to zucchini, which is precisely the right thing to do when there's not much broccoli around. But today, broccoli was cheap enough, which meant that the broccoli harvest was doing fine. The low price told you that, yes, you should go ahead and eat broccoli instead of zucchini for dinner tonight. And that's what you did.

Likewise, you didn't mess up Toyota's production line by not working for them. If you were so important, Toyota would have offered you a high enough wage to persuade you to go work for them. It would have made sense for them to pay you enormous sums of money to prevent millions of dollars' worth of lost cars. That they didn't offer you vast sums of money meant that you were not so critical to them.

And Pink Floyd didn't have to record their album in your basement. They found a recording studio somewhere. If they hadn't, and your basement had been essential to making *Wish You Were Here*, they would have offered you a high enough rent to make it worth your while to put up with all the noise. They wouldn't have let a few thousand dollars in extra rent cost them millions of dollars in album sales.

See how prices were pushing you in the right direction in all these instances? It'll take me two more chapters to prove it, but the prices got everything exactly right. They were silent conductors who synchronized you perfectly with the rest of society. Without your knowing it, they made you play all the right notes in the grand symphony of the economy—a symphony that neither you nor I can hope to comprehend.

Prices are perfect summaries that tell you everything you need to know and nothing you don't. The price of broccoli that you saw displayed in the grocery store told you everything you needed to know about the broccoli situation. If something were to happen so that you ought to eat less broccoli, all that would happen from your perspective is that the price of broccoli would rise to get you to eat less broccoli. The price won't tell you why you need to eat less broccoli. It may have been that swarms of broccoli-eating locusts swept through California, or that trucks carrying broccoli fertilizer ran off the road in China, or that Eddie next door decided to eat healthy and is really into broccoli now. The price doesn't tell you and you don't need to know. All you need to know is that you should eat less broccoli. And the price increase tells you to do that without filling you in on any of the unnecessary details.

Where do these amazing prices come from? How did the price of broccoli end up being $0.99 per pound and not $0.50 or $3.99? Why does a computer monitor cost $200 and not $20 or $20,000? Our first instinct is to think that the seller set that price. Broccoli is $0.99 per pound because the grocery store owner decided to write that on the price tag. A Samsung monitor costs $200 because a Samsung executive decided that. But while these are indeed the proximate reasons, they are ultimately a misleading description of how the price came about. Think about it this way: if the seller did indeed decide on the price, why didn't the seller charge even more? Surely every grocer would love to sell broccoli for $50 per pound. Samsung would love to sell their monitors for $3,000. Why didn't they? The answer is that the seller does not determine the price in isolation. An individual seller is just one small part of the equation. The price of a thing is actually set by billions of people who are in some way involved in producing or consuming that thing.

We'll get to the bottom of this mystery soon. But for now, let's just take a moment to appreciate the marvel that is the price tag. Whether affixed to broccoli at the grocery store, cranberry muffins at the bakery, one-bedroom apartments in Oslo, or nursing jobs in

Nigeria, price tags are powerful packets of information that masterfully conduct the grand symphony of production and consumption that is our economy.

# CHAPTER 8

# The Three Big Questions

We are closing in on the mystery of the market. How does the price emerge and get people to act in precisely the right way? What's the machinery behind the magic? To show you how it all works, I'm going to zoom in on one of the many millions of things that the economy has to do: the making and eating of cheeseballs.

In the vast economic ballet, there's a small part that's all about cheeseballs. A certain portion of the economy's resources should be used to produce a certain number of cheeseballs, which should then be consumed by certain people. This raises three big questions. First, how many cheeseballs should be produced and consumed? Second, how should the cheeseballs be produced—what labor and what capital should be used in what way to make them? Third, who should consume the cheeseballs?

In this chapter, we are going to work out the right answers to these three questions. That will tell us exactly what needs to be done. In the next chapter, we will see how centrally planned economies and free market economies get it done. This story about cheeseballs will apply equally well to everything that the economy produces and consumes, whether it's haircuts or helicopters or hip replacements.

So the three questions facing us are: *How many cheeseballs? How to produce them? Who should consume them?* I'm going to work backward, starting with the last question.

## QUESTION 1: WHO CONSUMES THE CHEESEBALLS?

The economy has produced a certain number of cheeseballs, say three hundred. Who should consume these three hundred cheeseballs? Some people don't like cheeseballs—clearly they should not eat one. But that still leaves a lot of people. Who among the many cheeseball lovers should eat a cheeseball?

How about we give the cheeseballs to the people who love cheeseballs the most? That seems pretty logical, but, surprisingly, it turns out to be wrong! Handing out cheeseballs on the basis of desire alone is inefficient. The correct way to hand out cheeseballs is on the basis of a somewhat different question: *how much other stuff are you willing to give up for a cheeseball?* How many shoes, watches, ice creams, and movies are you willing to forgo in order to eat a cheeseball? This is called the *willingness to pay* for a cheeseball.

We can measure willingness to pay in terms of ice cream cones and fur hats, but it's more convenient to just use dollars. If someone is willing to pay $7 for a cheeseball, that means he or she is willing to give up $7 worth of other stuff in order to eat a cheeseball.

Obviously, a person's willingness to pay for cheeseballs or anything else cannot exceed her entire wealth. In fact, it will be quite a bit less than that because she will want money left over for other things. This underscores the fact that willingness to pay depends not only on one's desire for something, but also on one's wealth. A rich tycoon with a passing interest in cheeseballs might be willing to pay more than a passionate cheeseball aficionado who just lost her job. I will explain soon why it is indeed willingness to pay, and not desire alone, that should determine who eats a cheeseball. But first, an aside on terminology.

Economists call the willingness to pay for something the *value* that the person places on that thing. It's a convenient term, and we're going to use it. But be warned that it's a misleading label that's liable to cause misunderstandings. According to this definition, rich people value clean air more than poor people because they're willing to pay more for it (because they can afford it). A beggar who is starving to death does not value food at all because he is not willing to give up anything for it (because he has nothing). Clearly the technical sense in which economists use the term "value" is at odds with our normal use of the term. It's important to keep in mind that in economics, the value of something to a person refers solely to the amount of other things that the person is willing and able to give up for it—nothing more.

Now back to the main story. I have made the controversial claim that the people who value cheeseballs the most should eat them. If there are three hundred cheeseballs, then the three hundred people who most value a cheeseball should eat them. It does not matter whether it was great desire or great wealth that made them so willing to pay. If the cheeseball goes to anyone else, the economy has malfunctioned. Let me explain why.

Consider the case of Lars and Lisa. Lars is a passionate cheeseball aficionado. But he is a graduate student on a meager stipend, subsisting on Ramen noodles and cabbage while writing his dissertation on dystopian visions in early modern Finnish poetry. Still, he loves cheeseballs so much that he is willing to pay $4 to eat one. He will have to cut back on cabbage for a week, but he's willing to do that for his cheeseball. Lisa likes cheeseballs too, though not nearly as ardently as Lars. But unlike Lars, she happens to be the CEO of a major corporation and has just received a $20 million bonus. Her desire may not be as great, but her bank account is greater, and she is willing to pay $50 for a cheeseball. This makes Lisa one of the top three hundred people in the willingness-to-pay-for-a-cheeseball rankings. Lars does not make the cut.

Now I have claimed that Lisa should eat a cheese-ball, and Lars shouldn't, even though Lars is the one who loves cheeseballs more. What would happen if we went by love instead of willingness to pay, and let Lars eat a cheeseball instead of Lisa? That would have been inefficient because the situation could have been unambiguously improved upon. Here's how: take the cheeseball from Lars and give it to Lisa and take $20 from Lisa and give it to Lars. Lisa would now be better off because she values the cheeseball she got more than the money she lost. Lars would also be better off because he values the money he got more than the cheeseball he lost. So it would have been possible to make both Lars and Lisa happier without hurting anyone else. A well-functioning economy cannot leave an opportunity like that on the table. So, in a well-functioning economy, Lisa will eat the cheeseball and Lars won't.

But that's not fair, you protest. Just because Lisa is rich, she should get the cheeseball on top of everything else she has? Not at all. While the cheeseball should go to Lisa, we are perfectly free to take other things from her. We can be as fair as we like by taking as much as we want from Lisa and giving it to Lars and other less fortunate people.

So we can say, without being hard-hearted, that the three hundred cheeseballs should go to those three hundred people who, because of great desire or great wealth, are willing to give up the most other stuff for it.

## QUESTION 2: HOW TO PRODUCE THE CHEESEBALLS?

How should the economy go about producing its cheeseballs? If three hundred cheeseballs are to be made, which of the economy's resources should go toward making them? What labor and what capital should be commandeered for the purpose? Should Jim make cheeseballs while Jody knits sweaters? Or should Jody make cheeseballs while Jim knits sweaters? Should the milk be stirred with wooden spoons in large aluminum vats or with aluminum spoons in small wooden vats?

To determine which resources should go toward making the cheeseballs, the right question to ask is: *how much other stuff is lost by using this resource to make cheeseballs instead?* If Jim is put to work making cheeseballs, he cannot knit sweaters. How many sweaters were lost? If an aluminum vat is being used to make cheeseballs, it cannot be used to make tomato sauce. How much tomato sauce was lost? This loss of sweaters and tomato sauce is called the *cost* of using the resource. It's what the economy loses by using the resource to make cheeseballs instead of something else. The cost of using Jim is three sweaters lost. The cost of using a large aluminum vat is four gallons of tomato sauce lost.

We can measure cost in terms of sweaters and to-mato sauce like this, but it's convenient to just use dollars. If the cost of a resource is $10, that means we'll lose $10 worth of other stuff by using that resource to make cheeseballs instead.

It follows, somewhat obviously, that however many cheeseballs are to be made, they be made with the lowest-cost resources. This is just another way of saying that the economy should give up as few other things as possible in order to make those three hundred cheeseballs. So start with the resource that costs the least—the least amount of sweaters and tomato sauce lost per cheeseball produced. Continue on to higher and higher-cost resources until we have enough to make three hundred cheeseballs. This way, the econo-my loses the least amount of sweaters and tomato sauce in pursuit of the needed cheeseballs.

Now for an aside on a potential source of confu-sion. In this story, the cost of making a cheeseball keeps rising as we produce more and more cheeseballs because we are forced to use costlier and costlier resources. But there's another force that I'm ignoring: making the first cheeseball involves some fixed costs—like learning the recipe and taking out the ingredients—that won't be incurred on subsequent cheeseballs. So subsequent cheeseballs are actually cheaper to produce than the first one. This is the economies of scale that we are all familiar with. But I'm ignoring this because fixed costs, though they may seem big to you and me, are still quite small on the scale at which most industries operate. To convince yourself of this, think about what would happen if the world had to produce twice as many cars as it currently does. Would it become cheaper to produce cars because the fixed costs are now spread over more cars? Or would it become more expensive because it's hard to procure the extra aluminum and rubber and skilled workers needed? More expensive, right? At these scales, the fixed cost savings are negligible compared to the scarcity of suitable resources. So we won't worry about it in our story.

## QUESTION 3: HOW MANY CHEESEBALLS?

The only remaining question is how many cheeseballs are to be made and eaten: Three? Three hundred? Three million?

Let's work this out one cheeseball at a time, starting with the first one. Should the economy make that first cheeseball? It will be made using the lowest-cost resources, so the economy will lose only $2 worth of other stuff. And it will go to the person who values it the most: Antwone, the billionaire cheeseball lover who is willing to give up $200 worth of other stuff for it. The cost of making the cheeseball is less than what Antwone is willing to give up for it. This means that we can take away enough from Antwone to adequately compensate whoever lost the sweaters and the pasta sauce, and still have plenty left over. So the first cheeseball is definitely a go.

What about the second cheeseball? This one will cost more ($3) because the lowest-cost resources were used up on the first cheeseball. The economy is forced to use higher-cost resources. More pasta sauce and sweaters will be lost for this cheeseball than for the first one. Moreover, it will go to someone who does not value it as much: Bethany, the millionaire cheeseball aficionado, who is willing to pay only $150 for a cheeseball. But the value still exceeds the cost, and so the second cheeseball is also a go.

And we keep going. With every additional cheeseball, the cost of making it rises and the value of consuming it declines. Eventually the cost will overtake the value. In other words, at some point, what society has to give up for one more cheeseball (the cost) is more than what it is willing to give up for it (the value). That is precisely where we must stop. If value is greater than cost for the three hundredth cheeseball, but not for the three hundred and first cheeseball, then the economy should produce three hundred cheeseballs and no more.

So there we have the answers to the three big cheeseball questions: *produce using the lowest-cost resources, give to the highest-value consumers, and stop when cost overtakes value.*

This is what is efficient. So this is what a well-functioning economy must accomplish when it comes to cheeseballs. And when it comes to bicycles and mattresses and Broadway plays and everything else that is produced and consumed in the economy.

# CHAPTER 9

# Planners and Markets at Work

Now we know what needs to be done: produce using the lowest-cost resources, give to the highest-value consumers, and stop when cost overtakes value. Let's see how this gets done by the central planning system and the free market system.

In a centrally planned economy, Cindy, the planner in charge of processed dairy, is put on the job. Cindy has her able assistants send out surveys to everyone asking how much stuff they are willing to give up for a cheeseball. She has other able assistants figure out the best way to make cheeseballs. They even experiment with new techniques that can potentially lower costs and improve flavor—these aren't lazy planners. Once all of this information is in, Cindy calculates correctly that the economy should produce three hundred cheeseballs. Letters are sent to the appropriate people to report for cheeseball-making duty. Big aluminum vats and wooden spoons are diverted from the tomato sauce division. Warehouses are secured and production begins. When the cheeseballs are ready, they are given to the three hundred people who indicated in the survey that they are the most willing to give up other stuff for a cheeseball. And that's how it all gets done in a centrally planned economy.

While the centrally planned economy is managed from above by Cindy and her assistants, the free market system takes a decentralized, grassroots approach that nevertheless manages to get things right without Cindy or anyone else in charge. How does this work? In the free market system, all labor and capital are owned by individuals who are free to do whatever they want with them. They can use them to make cheeseballs or tomato sauce or tennis rackets or throw them all away. It's their call. Cindy won't be telling them what to do. But people will naturally seek to do the best for themselves. And they are on the lookout for deals that they could make with others.

Antwone, the billionaire cheeseball lover, is willing to pay up to $200 for a cheeseball. Augustin, the cook, can rustle one up at a cost of just $2. There's a juicy deal to be made here: Antwone could pay Augustin $100 for a cheeseball. Both Antwone and Augustin will benefit from this deal and they're eager to shake hands on it. But how will they find each other in the teeming mass of humanity?

Enter the market—an institution that arose thousands of years ago to solve precisely this problem. The cheeseball market, located two blocks east of the town

square, is where everyone with an interest in cheeseballs shows up to strike deals with each other. Consumers like Antwone come looking to buy. Producers
like Augustin come looking to sell. So now the potential producers and consumers of cheeseballs are all in
one place, and they start talking to each other. Sellers
are looking to sell for as high a price as possible, and
buyers are looking to buy for as low a price as possible.
The negotiations begin.

Someone offers to buy a cheeseball for $1. At that
price, a lot of people want to buy a cheeseball because
they value it more than $1. There's a big *demand* for
cheeseballs at such a low price. But only those few
producers whose costs are below $1 are willing to sell
at that price. So there is little *supply* of cheeseballs from
sellers. Too many cheeseballs demanded by buyers, too
few supplied by sellers. Some buyers who would like to
buy a cheeseball won't get one.

A desperate buyer raises the offer to $2 in an at-
tempt to snag a scarce cheeseball for herself. At this
higher price, a few buyers drop out because the price is
now above their value. Conversely, a few sellers enter
because the price is now above their cost. So the
increase in price reduces the demand for cheeseballs
and increases the supply.

If, in spite of this, demand still outstrips supply, a
desperate buyer will raise the bid yet again in an
attempt to score that still-scarce cheeseball. Buyers

competing with each other push the price higher and higher. They will stop trying to outbid each other only when the price is high enough that the demand for cheeseballs equals the supply. At this price, enough buyers have been dissuaded, and enough sellers attracted, that there are enough cheeseballs for all buyers who are willing to pay the price. Let's say this happens when the price reaches $5 per cheeseball.

Now if the price goes above $5, the tables will be turned. There will now be more cheeseballs supplied than demanded. The heat will be on the sellers. They will have to compete with each other for scarce buyers. So they undercut each other, trying to attract a buyer for their cheeseball. This undercutting will stop only when the price falls far enough that enough sellers have been dissuaded, and enough buyers attracted, that demand again equals supply—i.e., when the price is back down to $5.

So it's all very neat and simple, really. The price must remain at $5 much like the natural height of a spring. Push it lower and it jumps back up; pull it higher and it snaps back down. If the price is below $5, competition between buyers outbidding each other to secure scarce cheeseballs pushes the price back up. If the price is above $5, competition between sellers undercutting each other to attract scarce buyers pulls the price back down. At the very special price of $5, there are exactly as many cheeseballs demanded as there are supplied. No buyer needs to outbid another, and no seller needs to undercut another. So that's the price at which cheeseballs end up getting traded. All producers whose costs are less than $5 will make and sell one. All consumers who value a cheeseball more than $5 will buy and eat one.

Now did all of this lead to the right things getting done? Were the cheeseballs produced using the lowest-cost resources, consumed by the highest-value consumers, and produced and consumed only as long as value exceeded cost? Yes, yes, and yes. Since only producers with costs below $5 made cheeseballs, only the lowest-cost resources were used. Since only consumers whose value exceeded $5 bought the cheeseballs, only the highest-value consumers ate them. Since all producers have a cost below $5, and all consumers have a value above $5, every cheeseball made and eaten had a value greater than its cost. So it was right to make and eat every one of them. But any additional cheeseball would have been made using resources that cost more than $5 (because lower-cost resources have already been used up), and would have been eaten by a consumer who values it less than $5 (because higher-value consumers have already eaten one). So no more should have been made and eaten. The market got everything exactly right! And it accomplished this without any supervision from Cindy and her assistants.

Note the central role played by the price in coordinating everything. It was that price of $5 that told everyone just what to do. It told lower-cost producers to produce, higher-value consumers to consume, and everyone else to stay away. You can see why prices have been likened to traffic signals for the economy— they tell people just what to do.

Prices are not determined by any one buyer or seller, but arise spontaneously from competition between all potential buyers and sellers. Competition between buyers keeps the price of cheeseballs from falling below $5 and competition between sellers keeps it from rising above $5. Everything from cell phones to lawn mowers to college tuition is priced in this way in a decentralized free market economy. Market forces jostle the price to that precise point where the supply from sellers equals the demand from buyers. That price was made by every person looking to buy or sell the thing. That's why it carries so much information and can direct the economy so well.

CHAPTER 10

# The Need for Incentives

In the last chapter, I described how central planning and the free market are supposed to work in principle. Central planning looks all neat and organized, while the free market looks a little chaotic. But in the laboratory of the real world, free markets have beaten central planning every time. Economies that adopted free markets—like Western Europe, North America, Australia, and the Asian "Tigers"—did well. Economies that attempted central planning—like China, India, Latin America, and the Soviet Union—did badly.

Particularly telling was when a country split in two, and each half tried a different system. At the end of World War II, Germany split into East and West. East Germany adopted central planning and failed. West Germany adopted free markets and prospered. It was a relatively clear comparison of the two systems. North and South Korea also provided a similar experiment, with a similar result in favor of free markets.

When planned economies switched to free markets, things usually improved quickly. But in some cases, the transition was slow and bumpy. The Soviet Union went through a particularly rough transition that had many economists wondering where the magic of the free market had gone. But keep in mind that the dismantling of the Soviet Union was not just an economic transition, but a full-blown political revolution as well. For obvious reasons, political revolutions get in the way of economic performance. A clearer picture is painted by countries that changed their economic system without undergoing political upheaval. China in the 1980s and India in the 1990s enacted pro-market policy changes while leaving their political structures in place—authoritarian rule in China and messy democracy in India. In both cases, under very different political arrangements, the results came in quick and clear: free markets worked better.

Why central planning fails and the free market succeeds comes down to incentives. Though central planning sounds reasonable in some ways, it breaks down in practice because it does not provide the right incentives to the people involved—not to the planners and not to the rest of us. Planners are not rewarded for the tremendous hard work involved in developing the right plan. Nor are they punished for doing things willy-nilly. So why should Cindy and her assistants make all that effort to get everything right? They don't. And it's not like we can solve this by offering them a bonus for a job well done. Remember that we have no idea what needs to be done. It's enormously difficult to calculate—that's why we need planners in the first place. The only feasible approach would be a system that does not require constantly monitoring the billions of decisions that need to be made every day throughout the vast economy.

Just as planners don't have an incentive to do their part well, the rest of us don't have an incentive to do our part well either. When Cindy's assistants call to find out how much we value that cheeseball, it's not in our best interest to answer honestly. Depending on how planners make their decisions, we might want to understate or overstate our value. It's a complicated process, and we have every incentive to lie and try to game the system. The only feasible approach would be a system that gets us to do the right thing based on information known only to us because it is in our own interest to do so.

These are all problems that get in the way of drawing up the master plan in the first place. When it comes to implementing the plan, a whole new slew of incentive problems crop up. How can Cindy get people to follow her plan? Cindy says you're supposed to show up at the farm and milk cows. But you'd rather play video games instead. How can Cindy get you to milk the cows? Put a gun to your head? Does Cindy even care? These are just not easy problems to solve.

In sharp contrast, the free market system gives everyone powerful incentives to do the right thing. It does not require second-guessing the billions of personal decisions made every day by every person in the economy. Each person decides and acts correctly based on the information known to them because it is in their own interest to do so. Sellers try to sell at the highest possible price, buyers try to buy at the lowest possible price. Fortunately, what emerges from these self-interested interactions is order, not chaos. The right things get done. The right number of cheeseballs get made using the right resources and get eaten by the right people.

The free market system works because it aligns the incentives of individuals with the interests of society as a whole. Central planning runs on the hope that people will, day after day, year after year, do the right things without the right incentives. But we know now that they don't—not enough to make it work. If people were all perfectly selfless, sure, it would have worked. We would all toil tirelessly for the greater good. But I, for one, am not perfectly selfless. Yes, I care about other people. I help old ladies put their suitcases in the overhead bin. You'll find me to be at least as nice as most people, and nicer than some. But I'm not perfectly selfless. If I were, I would never eat an ice cream cone. That money would have bought a gallon of milk for a malnourished child in Malawi. If my child were hungry, would I eat an ice cream cone? I do care about everyone. But I care more about myself and my own family and friends than I do about strangers. That is a fact of human nature. Any economic system that assumes otherwise is doomed to fail.

The free market system works by channeling our deep-seated selfishness into socially useful actions. The rules of the game prevent selfishness from being expressed as theft and murder and injury to others. We cannot just grab what we want from others because the rules protect every person's right to their own life, liberty, and property. Instead we have to persuade others to give us what we want by offering them what they want in return. It's quid pro quo: you scratch my back and I'll scratch yours. That's a powerful incentive scheme to get people to help each other. Why is the cook making cheeseballs for people he doesn't know? Why is the factory worker assembling cars for people she doesn't know? Why is the plumber fixing leaks for people he doesn't know? They're all doing nice things for strangers, but not out of kindness. They're doing it because, in return, they get to put food on their own table. Without that incentive, things fall apart.

# CHAPTER 11

# Fairness

The free market system works well. But it has one big shortcoming: while it is by nature efficient, it is not by nature equitable. Some people end up with bigger boats and more popcorn than others. If we want a fairer outcome, we must modify the system in some way to ensure that the economy's output is more evenly divided.

To address the problem, let's start with the root cause. Why, in a free market system, do some people get a bigger share of the economy's output than others? It's because they own more resources—they have more labor and capital than others. A person who can lift heavier rocks, or can design better software, or owns more land and factories will earn more and get a bigger share of the economy's output. Inequality in resources translates to inequality in outcomes.

This suggests a simple way to eradicate inequality: redistribute resources so that everyone has the same amount of labor and capital to begin with. That's a neat idea, but hard to implement. First, labor does not lend itself naturally to redistribution: how can you take away one person's dexterity and intelligence and give it to another? Redistributing capital is easier: just take Jack's tire factory and give it to Jill. Many revolutions have been built around this idea of taking land and factories from rich capital owners and giving them to the poor. But while a one-time redistribution of capital might work, it cannot be an ongoing policy. If we keep taking away people's capital and giving it to others, nobody will accumulate capital in the first place. Nobody will save up and build factories because they know that it will eventually be taken away from them.

A simpler and more practical approach than redistributing resources is to redistribute income, which is the ultimate goal of redistribution anyway. This can be easily done through the income tax system. Just set up a tax code where the rich pay more taxes, the middle class pay less taxes, and the poor pay negative taxes— meaning the poor receive money from the government rather than pay money to it. This will ensure that nobody falls below a minimum level of income. Something along these lines has been partially implemented in the United States through a program called the Earned Income Tax Credit, and has proved to be practical and effective.

Redistributing income from the rich to the poor is not without problems. It reduces incentives to work and save, so it will harm the economy some. But that does not automatically mean that it's not worth doing. It comes down to values. If we value a certain amount of equity—if we want to ensure that some people don't end up with too little—there just isn't a better alternative.

Other methods of redistribution are more harmful and less effective. Many bad laws originate from a desire to redistribute from rich to poor. Rent control laws are supposed to help poor tenants at the expense of rich landlords. Minimum wage laws are supposed to help poor workers at the expense of rich employers. Import tariffs on corn are supposed to help poor corn farmers at the expense of rich corn consumers. These sorts of regulations do much more damage than the blunted incentives of a negative income tax. Moreover, they have terrible aim. They can easily end up making the rich richer and the poor poorer. An import tariff might help a rich corn farmer at the expense of a poor corn consumer. Minimum wage laws might throw the lowest-skilled workers out of work (I will explain how in the next chapter). And here's a jaw-dropping example of rent control making the rich richer: Pop star Cyndi Lauper (of "Girls Just Wanna Have Fun") sued to have the rent on her upscale Manhattan apartment reduced from $3,250 per month to $508 per month under New York City's rent control laws. The court ordered her rent reduced to $989 a month.

A negative income tax is much better targeted to the poor for the simple reason that it's based directly on income. And it does its job with minimal damage to the economy and minimal bureaucracy. So if the goal is redistribution, then a negative income tax is the best tool we have for it.

My personal preference leads me to support income redistribution. I value living in a society where the less fortunate are taken care of. I would vote to tax the relatively well-off, including myself, and use those funds to help the poorest. But even if your values are different, you might still conclude that redistribution is politically necessary. Redistribution is going to happen one way or the other. The only question is, how? Will it show up as minimum wage laws, rent control, import tariffs, central planning, and bureaucratic welfare programs? Or will it show up as a simple, well-targeted, and easily administered negative income tax? On this matter, I think more people can agree.

A negative income tax will need to be supplemented by programs that provide extra help to those with special misfortunes—illnesses, disabilities, orphanhood, and so on. The precise details of a comprehensive safety net will necessarily be complicated. But the guiding principles should remain minimal bureaucracy and precise targeting of the needy. The powerful engine of a free market system, combined with a safety net built according to these principles, offers a better life for both rich and poor than the tangle of misguided rules, programs, and schemes that currently stifle our economies.

# CHAPTER 12

# Rules in the Way

No economy on earth is completely centrally planned or completely free market. The Soviet Union was mostly centrally planned, but allowed farmers and artisans to sell their goods in markets. Western economies are mostly free market, but have rules like minimum wage laws, rent control, and import restrictions that interfere with markets and constitute a limited form of central planning. In this chapter, I look at some of the rules that get in the way of markets and show how they cause problems.

The temptation to interfere in markets usually stems from a desire to help some segment of society. Minimum wage laws are meant to help low-wage workers. Rent control laws are meant to help tenants. Import restrictions on corn are meant to help corn farmers. The problem with these interventions is that while they help some people, they hurt others even more, and the economy as a whole is damaged. Moreover, the resulting redistribution could easily be perverse—taking from the poor and giving to the rich. If the goal is simply to help the needy, keep in mind that we have another option that does less damage and is better targeted: direct redistribution through a negative income tax. It takes from precisely the rich and gives to precisely the poor. Before interfering in markets, we must always consider whether our goals are better served by direct redistribution.

Rules that interfere with markets prevent people from making the deals that they want to make—you want to sell me a baseball bat and I want to buy it, but some rule says no. Since the engine of the free market system is people trying to make deals with each other, rules that get in the way of these deals cause inefficiencies. I'll show how various rules stop you from selling that baseball bat to me, and how this leads to problems.

Each section below focuses on a different rule. The sections are all organized the same way: you're about to sell me a baseball bat, the rule stops us, and bad things happen.

## OUTRIGHT BANS

You are about to sell me a baseball bat. But the rules forbid the buying and selling of baseball bats. An outright ban is the most complete way of killing a deal. I don't know of any outstanding bans on the buying and selling of baseball bats. But every country except Iran has banned the buying and selling of human organs. This means that those who need a kidney transplant can only hope that someone will be kind enough to give them a kidney for free. But such kindness has turned out not to be enough. Every year, thousands of people die waiting for a kidney. The rest of us go about our lives without offering to help. But if someone steps forward and offers to sell their kidney, and a desperate patient gladly accepts, we stop them.

It might make us uneasy that someone is prepared to sell his kidney. It's likely that the person is doing it because of financial difficulties. But if he's mentally sound and well informed about the risks and costs of giving up a kidney, his willingness to participate in the deal shows that he would rather have the money than the kidney. So blocking this transaction has hurt the potential seller, not helped him. And it has also hurt the potential buyer, who will die a needless death. Banning trade leads to errors; banning the organ trade leads to particularly tragic errors.

## PRICE CONTROLS

You are about to sell me a baseball bat for $80. But the rules forbid you from selling it for more than $60. Price controls like these have been popular throughout history. Nearly four thousand years ago, in one of the first codes of law written by humans, Hammurabi, king of Babylon, decreed that ferryboat rides be priced three gerahs per day. Fast forward two thousand years and we find Roman Emperor Diocletian insisting that haircuts not exceed two denarii. Today New York, Stockholm, Mumbai, and many other cities around the world have rent control laws that forbid rents from rising above some amount. Many countries have minimum wage laws that forbid wages from dipping below a certain level: in the United States, you cannot work for less than $7.25 per hour; in France, you have to charge at least 8.86 euros per hour; and in Lebanon, it has to be more than 675,000 Lebanese pounds per month.

Price controls are put in place to protect certain groups—tenants, in the case of rent control, and workers, in the case of minimum wage laws. The intentions might be noble. But, however well intentioned, price controls wreak havoc. Swedish economist Assar Lindbeck once said that "next to bombing, rent control seems in many cases to be the most efficient technique so far known for destroying cities."

Forcing the price of baseball bats down to $60 when the market price is $80 does damage on two fronts. At the price of $60, some producers find it no longer profitable to make bats since their costs are higher. They leave, reducing the supply of bats. Meanwhile, the lower price attracts new consumers who value bats at less than $80 but more than $60. The reduced supply and increased demand creates a shortage of baseball bats. Not everyone who is willing to pay $60 for a bat can get one. Lines form at sporting goods stores. A few lucky people who got in line early score a bat. The others go home empty-handed.

There are two wrongs that were done here—two sources of inefficiencies. First, on the production side, too few bats got made. Second, on the consumption side, those few bats might have gone to the wrong people: a person who valued the bat at $70 might have gotten one while a person who valued it at $500 might have gone home empty-handed.

What price control does to baseball bats, it also does to apartments. Rent control reduces the number of apartments by discouraging people from building new units or maintaining existing ones. Anyone who has tried to find an apartment in a rent-controlled city will attest to a severe shortage and a frustrating search. Plus, the wrong people get the scarce goods. A retiree will continue to live on in a prime Manhattan location close to a job he doesn't go to anymore because his controlled rent there is lower than the unregulated rent he can get in the suburbs. Meanwhile, someone who works in Manhattan will spend hours commuting from a distant suburb because she can't find an apartment close to work.

What price control does to baseball bats and apartments, it also does to labor. When the price of labor is forced above its natural market price through a minimum wage law, the demand for workers shrinks and the supply expands. Too many workers end up chasing too few jobs. Not everyone looking for a job will be lucky enough to land one, so some will become unemployed. A minimum wage law meant to help low-wage workers earn a better wage will end up putting some of them in the far worse position of not having a job.

Overriding market prices is a dangerous game fraught with unintended consequences. It tampers with the economy's traffic lights, which inevitably leads to errors. Inefficiencies pile up. If redistribution is the goal, then price controls are a bad way of going about it. They do a lot of damage, and can end up helping the rich and hurting the poor. We have a better tool for the job: direct redistribution through a negative income tax does less damage to the economy and is better targeted to the poor. Remember how rent control helped pop star Cyndi Lauper reduce the rent on her upscale apartment in Manhattan? A negative income tax would never have done that.

## TAXES

You are about to sell me a baseball bat. But the rules say that if we make this trade, we have to pay a $10 fee called a sales tax. Will we still go through with the deal? If I value the bat high enough, and the cost to you is low enough, we both stand to gain a lot. A $10 fee isn't going to stop us. But if we stand to gain less than $10, it's no longer worth the fee and the deal is off. So marginal deals get sunk, causing errors.

Though a tax does damage, the harm is less than what's caused by bans and price controls. A moderate tax on baseball bats will result in fewer bats produced and consumed—not zero as in a ban. The bats will be produced by the lowest-cost producers, as should be. And unlike with price controls, the bats will go to the people who value them the most, as should be. So the wounds inflicted by taxes are not as severe as those inflicted by price controls and outright bans, which are weapons of mass destruction. And unlike price controls and outright bans, taxes generate revenue to fund the government's expenditures. They serve a function for which there aren't good alternatives. As long as taxes are not excessive, we're just going to have to file them under the "necessary evil" category.

## INTERNATIONAL TRADE BARRIERS

You are about to sell me a baseball bat. But the rules say that I have to pay a $10 fee called an import duty, because you and I live in different countries. Political borders are meaningless lines when it comes to the economy. If it's a good idea for you to sell me a baseball bat, it doesn't become a better or worse idea if a political boundary happens to fall between where you and I live. That $10 import duty works much like a $10 sales tax would, discouraging trade in the same way and causing the same malfunctions.

By inhibiting trade between two countries, an import duty hurts some people and helps others. It turns out that in both countries, the harm outweighs the benefit. An import duty on baseball bats helps domestic producers who no longer have to compete with foreign producers. But it hurts domestic consumers who now face a higher price for baseball bats. The harm to consumers is greater than the benefit to producers, and the country as a whole is hurt. In the foreign country, it's the other way around—it's the producers who are hurt and the consumers who benefit. But here too, the gain to the winners is less than the loss to the losers, and the country as a whole loses. Both countries are net losers. This of course means that it's impossible for a country to use trade barriers to benefit itself at the expense of the other country.

The losses from trade barriers could be tolerated if they achieved a socially desired redistribution with the least damage possible. But they don't. Import restrictions redistribute arbitrarily and at great cost. Duties on agricultural products can make rich farmers richer while increasing food prices for everyone, including for the poorest of the poor. If redistribution is the goal, remember that we can directly redistribute through a negative income tax. This does much less damage, and the redistribution is from rich to poor, not the other way around.

## PROFESSIONAL LICENSING

You are about to sell me a baseball bat. But the rules say that unless you have a license allowing you to make and sell baseball bats, you can't do it. Ostensibly, this is to protect me from getting a lousy baseball bat. Barbers, florists, doctors, teachers, and hearing-aid fitters are some of the many professions that require a license to practice. Before accepting the argument that I need protection from ill-trained, charlatan florists, consider why I don't need protection from ill-trained, charlatan TV manufacturers. I don't need protection if I have a choice. If Sony makes a lousy TV, I'll buy one from Samsung instead. So either Sony makes a good TV, or it folds. Competition between producers is great consumer protection.

If professional licenses aren't really for protecting consumers, then what are they for? To solve the mystery, follow the breadcrumbs. Who clamors for instituting licensing requirements? Turns out, it's almost always the producers, not the consumers. It's the barbers and the florists and the teachers who demand licensing requirements, not their customers. And they want them because licensing reduces the competition they face. The more onerous the require-ments, the better. Once you have entered a profession, you want to pull the drawbridge shut behind you, preventing anyone else from entering and competing against you. Consistent with the true intent of the scheme, people who are already in the profession are typically exempt from new licensing requirements. So the whole thing works perfectly as a barrier against new entrants. The increased prices and reduced quality that the absence of competition leads to are the very antithesis of consumer protection.

These are just some of the vast thicket of rules that inhibit dealmaking, interfering with the core mechanism of the free market system. In Chapter 23, I will describe situations where free markets stumble and a little tinkering is in order. But the regulations I described in this chapter are almost always championed by those who don't comprehend the complexity of the economy and the impossibility of central calculation, by those who don't appreciate the ability of markets to get things right, and by those who stand to gain personally from bad laws that hurt the economy.

PART 2


SUBPLOTS

# CHAPTER 13

# Firms

When explaining how markets work, I described how owners of the appropriate labor and capital use their resources to make and sell cheeseballs to consumers. This happens through organizations called *firms*, which can be anything from big companies and corporations to small mom-and-pop businesses and one-person outfits.

A firm is a group of labor and capital owners who have gotten together to use their resources to produce and sell something. The firm collects labor and capital from these people, uses it to make cheeseballs, and sells the cheeseballs to consumers. The money obtained from selling the cheeseballs is funneled back to the owners of labor and capital in various ways. Labor is typically paid in the form of wages—that biweekly paycheck you get for working for a firm. Payments to capital are a bit more complicated. Depending on the arrangement, there are three ways that capital owners get paid—rent, interest, and profit. To see how the different arrangements work, let's look at a simple example.

Let's say you have $1,000 saved up. That's the capital you've got. Google wants to buy a $1,000 laptop for its newest employee. That's the capital it needs. You can give your capital to Google in one of three ways. First, you can use your $1,000 to buy the laptop yourself and rent it out to Google. Google pays you $50 a year as rent. Or you can lend your money to Google, which then uses the money to buy the laptop. Google pays you $50 a year as interest on the loan. Or you can give the money to Google in return for an ownership stake in the firm. Google uses the money to buy the laptop. As one of the owners of Google, you're entitled to a share of Google's profits (profit is what is left over after everyone else has been paid). Your share of the profits comes to $50 a year.

All of these transactions are equivalent in the sense that in each case you gave Google a $1,000 laptop and Google paid you $50 a year for it. The payment took the form of rent or interest or profit, but the transactions were the same in substance.

An interesting point worth noting is that we can be confident that all three arrangements will pay the same—in our example, $50 a year for $1,000 of capital. That's because if one paid less than the other, no one would participate in that arrangement. If interest were lower than rent, then no one would loan their money to Google. Instead, they would buy the capital themselves and rent it out to Google. If profit were lower than interest, then no one would want to own Google. Instead, they would only lend to it. All three arrangements would have to have the same terms for all three to be in use. (Actually, since a firm's profits are uncertain, expected profits will have to be a bit higher to compensate for the additional risk. But let's ignore that wrinkle.) So the rental rate, the interest rate, and the profit rate all have to be the same. They are just different expressions of one underlying rate—the rate of return on capital. In our example, that rate was 5% per year. This is about what it normally is in the real world, give or take a few percentage points.

But to return to our main point, the firm is a group of owners of labor and capital using their resources to produce some output, selling it, and collecting the resulting revenue. Firms can be big or small, formal or informal. I'm writing this book on my computer at home. So I'm running a small firm that hires my own labor and capital to produce an output (this book) that my firm—meaning, I—will try to sell. All proceeds, if any, will come back to me as the sole owner of all the labor and capital used. This is a small, informal firm. At the other end of the spectrum are giant corporations like Microsoft, ExxonMobil, and Toyota. They may look imposing, but they really are just larger versions of my little book-producing firm, involving many more owners of labor and capital.

## CHAPTER 14

# Eliminating Competition

Competition is the life force of the free market system. Not competition in the sense of a race where the winner gets a trophy and everyone else loses. Rather, in the sense that I can't stick you with a lousy deal since you are free to deal with others. Competition between sellers keeps prices from rising too high. Competition between buyers keeps prices from falling too low. The resulting in-between price is perfect in the sense that it gets everyone to do the right thing—the right producers produce, the right consumers consume, and everyone else stays away. Competition is essential to the story.

Eliminating your competition, while bad for society, is good for you personally. If you eliminate competition from your fellow buyers, you can buy at a lower price. If you eliminate competition from your fellow sellers, you can sell at a higher price. There are two ways to get rid of your competition: kill them, or join them.

The "kill them" strategy is to erect barriers to prevent your competitors from entering the market. I mentioned earlier how professional licensing requirements are used to prevent new people from coming in and competing with those who are already in the business. International trade barriers are another example: import duties prevent foreign producers from competing with domestic producers.

But the absolute best way to kill off the competition is to get a law passed that allows only you to buy or sell something. In one masterstroke, you would have dealt the deathblow to your entire competition. A law granting you the exclusive right to sell something gives you a *monopoly* on that market. A law granting you the exclusive right to buy something gives you a *monopsony* on that market. Every seller would love to be a monopoly, and every buyer would love to be a monopsony. It's hard to get the gig, but every once in a while someone does land one. In 1600, Queen Elizabeth I gave the British East India Company a monopoly to trade with "all countries east of the Cape of Good Hope and west of the Straits of Magellan" for fifteen years. In 1798, the state of New York gave a Mr. Robert Fulton exclusive rights to provide steamboat traffic on the Hudson river for thirty years. Patenting a new invention is a common way to get a temporary monopoly. If you invent a new drug and patent it, you will be the only one allowed to sell it for a period of time (twenty years in the United States).

If you can't kill the competition, you can try to join them instead. This involves making a pact with your fellow sellers not to undercut them, or with your fellow buyers not to outbid them. This is called *colluding*. A group of producers who agree not to compete with each other in an effort to prop up the price is called a *cartel*. Most countries outlaw such behavior, so company executives trying to collude have to wear fake beards and meet in smoke-filled basements. But some producers operate above the law. The most famous cartel is the Organization of Petroleum Exporting Countries (OPEC). This is a group of oil-producing countries that openly collude to keep oil prices high. And because they are sovereign countries, there is no law that says they can't.

Legal or not, it's hard to collude successfully for long. Each member of a cartel has a strong incentive to leave the cartel, undercut the cartel price, snag all the customers, and rake in all the profits. This temptation is naturally hard to resist. Moreover, the lure of easy profits attracts potential new entrants. These forces combine to make cartels inherently unstable. Without the help of regulation, competition is hard to snuff out. As the economist George Stigler put it, "Competition is a tough weed, not a delicate flower."

The examples I gave all involve producers, not consumers, trying to eliminate their competition. This was no accident. Producers tend to be much more energetic about protecting their interests than consumers. That's because we all tend to produce one thing but consume many things. If you eat soybeans, you could try to collude with your fellow soybean consumers to lower the price of soybeans, or lobby your congressman to erect export barriers. Let's say these efforts finally pay off and you manage to cut the price of soybeans in half. What do you gain? A dollar or two on your weekly grocery bill, that's all. It's just not worth the trouble.

On the other hand, if you are a soybean farmer, then soybeans are your life. A doubling of the price of soybeans would make you rich, and a halving would be disastrous. So it makes sense for you to join forces with your fellow soybean farmers and seek protection for your industry. You might try to collude with them to raise prices. You might lobby your local congressman to erect import barriers or call for new soybean farmer licensing requirements. This is why most regulations protect producers at the expense of consumers. The gain is concentrated on a few producers, who are moved to vigorous action, while the loss is dispersed across many consumers, who barely notice.

# CHAPTER 15

# Investing

In the beginning, all capital comes from nature: the fertile land, the fish in the sea, the coal in the ground. When Max washed up on the island, there were coconut trees and farmable land and trout-filled streams waiting for him. At first, these natural resources were his only capital. But over time, Max can add to or subtract from his initial stock of capital. If he makes a fishing rod, his capital is augmented—that fishing rod will help him produce output in the future. If he cuts down a tree to build a fire, his capital is depleted—that missing tree will hinder his ability to produce output in the future. In this way, the stock of capital changes over time. Today's choices determine tomorrow's capital.

An economy's output on any given day can be divided into *consumption* and *investment*. Investment is something that adds to the stock of capital. That fishing rod that Max made was an investment. Building a cabin, sewing a shirt, tilling the soil—these are all investments because they will help Max tomorrow. Consumption, on the other hand, refers to things that are enjoyed and used up today—gathering berries for today's dinner, building a fire to keep warm, watching the sunset. These won't be around to help Max tomorrow.

One of the most important decisions facing Max is how much of today's output should go toward consumption and how much toward investment. Should he spend the day making a fishing rod, or catching fish for today's dinner? If he makes the fishing rod, he eats less today but more tomorrow. If he catches fish for today's dinner, he eats more today but less tomorrow. Every economy faces this choice every day. Should the economy use its scarce resources to manufacture machines, construct buildings, and develop a cure for cancer? The fruits of these activities lie in the future. Or should it use its resources to make and eat pancakes today? The right balance between consumption and investment depends on how much people are willing to give up today in order to get more tomorrow. If they are willing to give up a lot today for a little more tomorrow, then the economy should be consuming little and investing lots. Conversely, if they are willing to give up a lot tomorrow for a little more today, then the economy should be consuming lots and investing little. It all depends on what people want.

In a planned economy, central planners will do all the calculations and conclude that people should consume this much and invest that much. In the free market economy, people are, as always, left to their own devices. Each person decides how much to personally consume and invest.

Let's say your income this year was $50,000. You spent $40,000 on rent and food and vacations and movies. This was your consumption—it's gone. You saved the remaining $10,000. This was your investment—it will be around to help you next year. The $10,000 you saved adds to your personal stock of capital. You can hold this extra capital and rent it out to firms in different ways. You can buy a building or machine directly and rent it out to a firm, in which case you get paid in the form of rent. Or you can loan the money to a firm, which then uses that money to buy the building or machine it needs. In this case you get paid in the form of interest. (This loan can be made directly by buying the firm's bonds, or indirectly by putting the money in a bank which then lends that money to the firm.) Or you can use the money to buy the firm's stock, which makes you a part-owner of that firm. The firm uses your money to buy the building or machine, and you get paid by way of profits. One way or the other, that $10,000 you did not consume becomes additional capital that you now own and rent out.

Most economies save and invest a portion of their output, thereby growing their capital and output over time. In 2010, the United States saved about an eighth of its output, Germany saved about a quarter, and

China saved about half. All else equal, the more an economy saves and invests, the faster it grows.

A common misconception is that if everyone saves their money instead of spending it, the economy will suffer. The concern is, who's going to buy all the stuff that's being produced? The fallacy here is to think that output can only be consumption goods. Output can also be investment goods. When people save, they are simply purchasing investment goods instead of consumption goods. The hamburger not bought is the sewing machine bought. So greater saving leads not to an idling economy, but to an economy busy manufacturing sewing machines, constructing factories, and developing a cure for cancer.

# CHAPTER 16

# The Total Output of an Economy

Let's take a look at the total output of an economy over some period of time, say a year. This tells us how well the economy did during that time. Did we catch a lot of fish and knit a lot of socks? The obvious way to measure this is to make an exhaustive list of everything that the economy produced that year: forty tons of salmon, eighty thousand heads of broccoli, six million pairs of socks, and so on. But such a list will overwhelm our minds. So to summarize it, we translate everything into dollar values, add it all up, and say that the economy produced $53 billion worth of stuff last year. This number is called the *Gross Domestic Product* (G.D.P.) of the economy for that year.

In 2010, the United States produced about $15 trillion worth of stuff, which comes to about $48,000 per person. Bangladesh produced about $280 billion worth of stuff—this is in U.S. dollars, adjusted for price differences between the two countries so that it can be directly compared to the U.S. figures. This comes to about $1,700 per person, or 1/28th of what the American produced. The average American managed to produce twenty-eight times as much stuff as the average Bangladeshi!

Let's see what the average American did with all the stuff they produced. About $33,900 worth of stuff (71%) went toward consumption—haircuts and dinners and trips. About $6,000 (13%) was investment—new buildings and equipment and research. About $9,800 (20%) was taken by the government as taxes, part of which they will consume (parades) and part of which they will invest (highways). Wait a minute—that adds up to $49,700 (104%). The average American produced only $48,000. Where did the extra $1,700 come from? How could Americans have consumed and invested more than they produced? You guessed it—they borrowed the difference from other countries like China. They'll have to pay it back with interest at some point. But in 2010, they got to spend more than they produced.

This borrowing from other countries shows up as a trade deficit with those countries. In 2010, the average American bought about $7,700 worth of stuff from foreigners (imports), but sold them only $6,000 worth of stuff (exports). So $1,700 worth of stuff was bought on credit and will have to be paid for later. A trade deficit—whether for a country or a village or a person—is just another word for borrowing. So the consequences of a trade deficit are the same as the consequences of borrowing. And that depends very much on whether you consume or invest the borrowed money. If you borrow to consume more today (eat hot dogs), you will have less tomorrow. But if you borrow to invest more today (build a factory), you may have more or less tomorrow depending on whether the value of the factory exceeds the debt you have to repay. So looking at borrowing in isolation is meaningless. Rather, you want to look at the difference between the amount invested and the amount borrowed. If you borrow $2,000 and invest $10,000, you will be in better shape tomorrow than if you borrow nothing but invest only $1,000.

In that spirit, note that in 2010 the average American invested $6,000, but borrowed only $1,700 from the rest of the world, giving her a net savings of $4,300. If that number were higher, she would have had more tomorrow but less today. If it were lower, she would have had more today but less tomorrow. The right balance between consuming and investing—between pleasure today and pleasure tomorrow—depends on personal preferences. But I, for one, am always surprised at how little people choose to save—how willing they are to sacrifice tomorrow for today!

# CHAPTER 17

# Budget Deficits

A government, like the rest of us, can spend more than it earns by borrowing the difference. This is called running a *budget deficit*. A government's main source of income is the taxes it collects from its people. If the government's expenses exceed the taxes it collects, it has to either raise taxes or borrow to fund the difference. So should it raise taxes or should it borrow? Does it even matter? To find out, let's look at an example.

Suppose the government needs a hundred pineapples to feed its soldiers. It can fund this expense by collecting a plain old tax: corner Joey and tell him to hand over a hundred pineapples. It's a straightforward strategy, but it upsets Joey, who vows never to vote for this government ever again. Might there be another way to take Joey's pineapples without riling him up so much? Indeed, there is: borrow Joey's pineapples. The government still gets the hundred pineapples from Joey, just like with the tax. The only difference is that it has promised to give him back the pineapples next year, with interest. So Joey's not upset anymore. Everybody's happy.

Next year comes around, and Joey shows up to collect the hundred and five pineapples he's owed (the hundred pineapples he lent, plus five pineapples as interest). The government now needs a hundred and five pineapples to pay Joey off. It could get those pineapples by taxing someone, but taxing hasn't become any more appealing now than it was last year. So it borrows a hundred and five pineapples from Judy to pay Joey. And the year after that, it borrows a hundred and ten pineapples from Jane to pay Judy. This goes on forever. Every time someone is owed pineapples, the government simply borrows from someone else to pay its debt. No one's upset.

But focus on what matters, which is how many pineapples people lost. In the first year, Joey lost a hundred pineapples. Every year thereafter, pineapples are simply being reshuffled across people. The second year, Joey got a hundred and five of Judy's pineapples. The third year, Judy got a hundred and ten of Jane's pineapples. And so on. There's a law of conservation of pineapples at work here. The government needed a hundred pineapples the first year and none thereafter. So people had to give up a hundred pineapples the first year and none thereafter. Whether the government got those pineapples by taxing people once or by borrowing forever, the law of conservation of pineapples meant that people lost a hundred pineapples the first year and none thereafter.

What's fascinating—and insidious—about this is that no one noticed that the government took their pineapples. Ask people to raise their hand if they lost any pineapples, and not a single hand goes up. Someone is always short a few pineapples, yes, but they know that they will get them back tomorrow with interest. And they will—from someone else's stash of pineapples.

Most governments in the world run large budget deficits and accumulate massive debts. It's easy to see why—it's a clever way to take pineapples from people without them noticing. People don't realize that those pineapples are gone forever. With taxing, they notice; with borrowing, they don't.

One way to really see that what the government borrowed is gone forever is to recognize that the only way the government can pay back what it owes people is to take it from the people in the first place. Let's say the government has borrowed $30,000 from each person in the country. Everyone is pleased that they have $30,000 saved up and invested in government bonds. They feel rich—they'll be getting lots of money tomorrow from the government. Hooray! But wait— the only way the government can pay them that money is by taking that money from them in the first place. It will need to collect $30,000 per person to pay the $30,000 per person that it owes. So nobody really has $30,000, do they? It's imaginary.

To avoid this deceptive thinking, we must subtract our government's debt from our wealth, because what our government owes is ultimately our responsibility. As of March 2012, the United States government owed $10.85 trillion. This works out to about $35,000 per person, or $140,000 for a family of four. So if a family of four living in the United States has saved $150,000, it really has only $10,000 left after its share of the government debt is subtracted. It's stunning, but true. Your credit card debt is probably small potatoes compared to what you owe on your government debt.

Budget deficits would have been a harmless alternative to taxes if we all realized that our government's debt is our own debt, knew that we were poor, and acted accordingly. But we don't. We are tricked into thinking that we are richer than we are. So we act rich, spend too much, and end up poorer than we otherwise would have been. Our imaginary wealth leads us astray. That's the damage done by the black-magic wand of budget deficits. The spell it casts, while pleasant, does real harm.

# CHAPTER 18

# Money and Inflation

An alien from a distant galaxy peers through a telescope and sees Eduardo buying his morning cup of coffee. The alien watches as the owner of the café hands Eduardo a cup of coffee and, in return, Eduardo hands her some crumpled pieces of paper. The alien is puzzled. The café owner just gave Eduardo something useful and, in return, she got some useless pieces of paper. Why would she agree to this lousy deal?

The tattered pieces of paper were dollar bills. And, yes, they are inherently useless. But the café owner is happy to take them because she knows that she too can exchange them later for useful things like staplers and iPads. The value of those pieces of paper comes purely from the confidence that they can be traded later for useful things. If, for some reason, people lose that confidence, as does sometimes happen, they will stop accepting dollar bills for coffee and staplers and iPads.

Dollar bills are an example of *money*. Money exists solely to make it easy to trade with others. To see how useful money is, imagine a world where money has not been invented. If Eduardo wants to buy a cup of coffee from the café owner, he has to pay her in staplers, because that's what she wants. But what if Eduardo is an artist and has only paintings to sell? Well, then he needs to find someone who is looking to trade a stapler for a painting. He could then exchange his painting for a stapler with this person, and then come back and exchange the stapler for coffee with the café owner. This system, where people trade without using money, is called a *barter* system. While possible in principle, it's awfully inconvenient in a complex modern economy. That's why people invented money. That way Eduardo can trade money for coffee with the café owner now, and the café owner can later trade that money for a stapler with someone else. Money simply facilitates our transactions.

Money is so useful that in World War II prisoner-of-war camps where cash wasn't available, prisoners began using cigarettes as money. Peppercorn, alcohol, cowry shells, gold, and silver are some of the other items that have been used as money at one time or another. But nowadays we mostly use pieces of paper like U.S. dollars and Chinese yuan.

Money that has some intrinsic value, like cigarettes and peppercorn and gold, is called *commodity money*. Dollars, yuan, pesos, and other paper money have no intrinsic value and are called *fiat money*. The advantage of paper money over commodity money is convenience. It's easier to carry around dollars and pesos than gold coins and peppercorn. That's why modern societies have abandoned commodity money in favor of paper money.

Technically speaking, anyone can issue paper money. I can print out pieces of paper that say "One Ben Mathew Dollar" in fancy font, and we could all use those for our transactions. But you won't accept it when I try to buy something from you, because you are not confident that others will accept it when you try to buy something from them. The Ben Mathew dollar suffers from a lack of confidence. For whatever reason, we have more confidence in the pieces of paper printed by our governments. So we end up using United States dollars and Japanese yen and Nigerian nairas for our transactions, though fundamentally they are no different from Ben Mathew dollars.

The confidence that people place in their governments' paper money cannot be taken for granted. Governments can nurture that confidence, or they can abuse it for short-term gain by indiscriminately printing more paper money to finance their expenses, thereby devaluing the currency and discouraging its use. Usually they abuse people's confidence only a little, and everything putters along just fine. But every once in a while, in times of great economic or political turmoil, people lose confidence in the pieces of paper printed by their government and will refuse to accept them as payment. Instead, they may use cigarettes or cognac or a foreign government's currency for their transactions.

During the breakup of the Soviet Union in the 1980s, people in Moscow began using cigarettes and U.S. dollars instead of the Soviet ruble. During a crisis in Zimbabwe in 2008, people lost faith in the currency printed by their government and began using foreign currencies instead. The government eventually abandoned the national currency, and has yet to issue a new one, because the confidence that was lost has yet to return.

To understand how money is introduced and managed, let's walk through what a government needs to do to get a currency up and running from scratch. Imagine an economy where money has not yet been adopted. People trade using the barter system—exchanging avocados for hats and so on. Finally, their ruler, the Great Pharaoh, succumbs to years of nagging from his finance minister and introduces a currency that he decides to call the pharon, after himself. He prints out a million slips of paper with the words "one pharon" written on them. Being a fair fellow, he decides to divide up the pharons equally between all his subjects, which works out to ten pharons per person. The next day, everyone finds ten crisp new pharon bills in their mailboxes. From then on, they happily trade with each other using their pharons.

Note how the Great Pharaoh did not say how many pharons an avocado or a hat should go for. Indeed, he cannot. He got to decide how many pharons to print and release into the economy. Whether a pharon will end up being worth one avocado or fifty will now be determined in the market for pharons.

Suppose people decide that they need to keep twenty avocados' worth of pharons on hand for their trades. So if a pharon is worth one avocado, they will need twenty pharons. If a pharon is worth two avocados, they will need only ten pharons. And so on. This means that if a pharon is worth less than two avocados, everyone will try to buy more pharons because the ten pharons they got in the mail are not enough to buy twenty avocados. Competition between people trying to buy more pharons pushes up the value of pharons. Conversely, if a pharon is worth more than two avocados, everyone will try to sell some of their pharons because the ten pharons they got in the mail are more than what they need to buy twenty avocados. Competition between people trying to sell their pharons pushes down the value of the pharons. The only value at which people stop trying to outbid or undercut each other is when one pharon is worth exactly two avocados. So we end up with one pharon being worth two avocados, i.e., a price of half a pharon per avocado. This is the *price level* of the economy.

You can see that the price level of the economy is directly proportional to how many pharons the Great Pharaoh mailed out. If he had mailed out twice as many pharons, prices would have been exactly twice as high.

Right now, where I live, broccoli costs $1.50 per pound, a Toyota Camry costs $25,000, and a plumber charges $120 to fix a leak. If the U.S. government decided to double the amount of dollars circulating in the economy, all of these prices would double as well: broccoli would cost $3 per pound, a Toyota Camry would cost $50,000, and a plumber would charge $240 to fix a leak.

A high or low price level is neither good nor bad—it affects nothing of substance. Suppose the Great Pharaoh had mailed out twice as many pharons to his subjects. Prices for everything would be double, but people would have twice as many pharons. So their pharons will buy the same number of avocados as before. People will carry out the same deals with each other, just with twice as many pharons as they otherwise would have.

Most countries print more money every year, causing price levels to rise over time. For example, in the United States, prices doubled over the last twenty-four years. In India, they doubled over the last eleven years. This general rise in prices is called *inflation*. Note that inflation does not refer to the rise in price of one thing relative to another. It refers to a rise in the average price of all things.

Nobody likes inflation. People are always complaining about how things are so much more expensive now than they were a decade or two ago. They feel that without inflation, their lives would have been much better because they could have afforded more things. But this is not correct. Inflation causes all prices to rise proportionally, including the prices of the labor and capital from which people derive their incomes. So inflation raises people's incomes precisely as much as it raises the prices of carrots and condos, leaving unchanged what they can and cannot afford. Inflation is perfectly harmless in this sense.

But inflation can be harmful in other ways, especially when it's extreme. Extreme inflation—with prices doubling in a matter of days or weeks—is called *hyperinflation*. In October 1923, prices in Germany were doubling every four days. In November 2008, prices in Zimbabwe were doubling every day. When inflation gets this high, people won't want to keep money in their wallets and purses. As soon as they get their paychecks, they rush to spend all their money before prices rise. On paydays during the German hyperinflation, schoolteachers would meet their relatives during recess to hand over their paychecks so that the money could be spent immediately. It would lose too much value by evening. The whole purpose of money is to make it easy to trade with others. It does not serve that purpose well if people cannot carry it around in their wallets and purses.

Another inconvenience is the constant updating of prices that becomes necessary. Restaurant menus and store price tags have to be reprinted every few days or even hours to reflect newer, higher prices. That's a lot of time and energy and paper wasted.

But perhaps the greatest harm inflicted by hyperinflation is a most brutal redistribution from one segment of the population (the lenders) to another (the borrowers). Let's say you've saved your whole life and are about to retire. You've deposited your savings in the bank or invested them in bonds. Either way, you lent your money to someone, and they promised to pay you back a certain amount of money in the future. If inflation is lower than expected, that money will translate to more stuff than expected—good news for you and bad news for the borrower. If inflation is higher than expected, that money will translate to less stuff than expected—bad news for you and good news for the borrower.

Now imagine it's January 1922, and you're a German retiree whose life savings are in the bank. Neither you nor anyone else knows that a loaf of bread that costs 163 marks today will cost 200 billion marks by November of next year! Inflation will soon wipe out pretty much the entire value of your savings. Of course, those who borrowed your money will be delighted that the value of their debt has been wiped out as well. But these wrenching redistributions sow misery and spark social unrest. In Germany's case, it wound up strengthening the Nazi Party.

Money is a necessary device for the proper functioning of an economy, and managing it responsibly is not rocket science. Governments need only to refrain from printing so much more money that it leads to large and violent bouts of inflation. Zero inflation, or at most a small, stable, and predictable inflation, is the goal.

But governments have a hard time resisting the urge to print more money. Why? Because, unlike the Great Pharaoh, who mailed the newly-printed pharons to his subjects, our governments like to keep their newly-printed pounds and pesos and use them to fund their expenses—building bridges, paying government employees, and so on. So printing money is a source of income for the government. It's a substitute for taxes. Governments like to avoid taxes as much as possible because people notice and protest. Whenever possible, they prefer sneakier ways of taking our money. In the last chapter, I described how borrowing—i.e., running budget deficits—is one way of doing this. Printing money and keeping it is another: people won't miss what they never got in the first place.

# CHAPTER 19

# Banks

Banks play a critical role in the economy. The havoc caused by the banking crisis of 2008 shows just how important they are. So what are banks, how do they work, and what are they good for?

Once upon a time, banks were just fortified warehouses where you could keep money safe from robbers. When you got money from your employer or your tenant or whoever, you would take it to the bank and give it to the teller, who would put it in a great big vault in the basement. When you needed money to pay the plumber or the grocer or whoever, you would go back to the bank and ask the teller to get your money out of the vault. Obviously, the bank would charge you a monthly fee for this service.

Centuries passed. Then one day, Archie, the owner of one of these warehouse banks, had an idea that would change banking forever. He noticed that there was always a pile of money sitting in his bank's vault. On a typical day, Archie's vault held about $5 million of customer deposits. Some days, customers deposited more money than they withdrew and the vault would hold as much as $5.5 million. Other days, customers withdrew more money than they deposited and the vault would hold as little as $4.5 million. But unless all of the bank's depositors decided to withdraw all of their money at the same time—an extremely unlikely scenario—the vault would always hold some money. Looking over past records, Archie confirmed that the lowest the deposits had ever fallen over the last twenty years was $4.43 million. He became convinced that there was just no way his deposits would fall below $4 million.

This meant that Archie could take $4 million out of the vault and loan it out and collect interest on it, without in any way inconveniencing his depositors. Life for his depositors would go on exactly the same as before—they could still deposit their money whenever they wanted and withdraw it whenever they wanted. So they wouldn't object, especially if Archie eliminated the monthly fee he had been charging them and, instead, passed along some of the interest he earned on their deposits.

Turns out customers loved this idea. They allowed banks to loan out their deposits in return for free checking accounts and interest payments. This meant a crucial change in the role of banks. Banks were no longer just warehouses to store people's money. They had become intermediaries through which people loaned their money to others. This is why banks play such an important role in the economy. They are vehicles through which we rent our capital to others. When banks get into trouble, capital doesn't flow to where it should, and that can gum up the economy pretty good.

This new species of bank is called a *fractional reserve bank* because it keeps only a fraction of its depositors' money in the vault—the rest has been loaned out. If too many depositors show up at the same time to withdraw their money, the bank won't be able to honor its promise to return depositors' money when asked. A bank in this position is said to have *failed*. Failure does not mean that the depositors' money is lost forever. It just means that the money is temporarily unavailable since it has been loaned out, and will eventually return when all the loans are paid back.

Virtually all of the banks we have now are fractional reserve banks. The fact that these banks don't keep enough money in their vaults to pay all their depositors is a bit worrying, isn't it? That worry turns out to be a problem. Archie is confident that, under normal circumstances, his depositors will not all want to withdraw their money at the same time. But once he starts lending out their deposits, people know that he doesn't have enough money in his vault to pay everyone. Under normal circumstances, this does not cause much concern. But what if you, having deposited money in Archie's bank, hear rumors that other people, worried about something, are taking their money out?

Just to be safe, you run to the bank to withdraw your deposits before the bank runs out of cash. Seeing you run, others run too. Soon, all of Archie's depositors are standing in line to take their money out and the bank runs out of cash. Archie is forced to turn his depositors away empty-handed. This is called a *run on the bank*. Even an unfounded fear of failure can precipitate a run and cause a bank that had been perfectly healthy in the morning to fail by afternoon.

Fractional reserve banks are therefore always in a precarious position. They rely on their depositors' confidence, which is fragile. So bank runs and bank failures used to happen frequently. The problem was eventually solved by governments stepping in and insuring bank deposits: if a bank failed, the government promised to give depositors back their money. That's a promise the government can credibly keep because it will never run out of money. It can always print more if needed. So depositors stopped worrying about bank failures. They didn't bother to rush to their bank when they heard rumors. So the banks stopped failing in the first place. It's because of deposit insurance that you and I are not worried right now about the safety and accessibility of the money that we have in our bank accounts.

But deposit insurance does not cover the entire banking system. There are some institutions that don't directly take in deposits, but are kind of like banks in that they borrow from one party and invest in another—like a traditional bank borrows from its depositors and invests in loans. These bank-like institutions will fail if people stop loaning them money, just as traditional banks will fail if depositors stop giving them their money.

In September 2008, one such institution, the Wall Street firm Lehman Brothers, collapsed and set off a global financial crisis. The fundamental source of Lehman's troubles was that it had made bad investments. There had been concerns about the firm for over a year. But the startling speed with which the firm crashed when it did was because long-simmering concerns coalesced into a run on the firm. Worried about Lehman's prospects, some people stopped loaning it money and otherwise trading with it. Frightened, others stopped as well. In the blink of an eye, a 158-year-old Wall Street giant collapsed.

Panic set in. People were afraid to lend their money to anyone, not knowing who would fall next. Perfectly healthy firms ran the risk of collapsing because they could not get loans. Governments across the world had to step in and make all sorts of promises to quell the panic and reinstate the confidence on which our banking system relies.

# CHAPTER 20

# Central Banks

Central banks are a powerful arm of the government. They go by different names in different countries: Bank of England, Reserve Bank of India, the Federal Reserve System of the United States, and so on. They have two main responsibilities: manage the country's money supply, and prevent banking crises by lending to banks when they get in trouble.

Managing the country's money supply involves deciding how much money to print and circulate. The central bank's authority over this process is the primary source of its power. Most countries have set it up so that their central bank does not answer directly to presidents and parliaments. This shields them a little from short-term political pressure to print more money to finance each year's budget shortfall.

A central bank can change the amount of money in the economy in different ways. To increase the money in our hands, it could just print up a bunch of dollar bills and mail them to us. But of course it does not do this. Instead, it uses the newly-printed dollar bills to buy stuff from us. That way, we still end up with the new dollar bills, but the government also gets something from us.

The things that central banks like to buy from us are not wheat and shampoo, but financial assets like bonds, gold, and foreign currencies. Naturally, when someone is spending billions of dollars to buy something, it pushes up the price of that thing. So the buying spree by the central bank increases the price of bonds, gold, foreign currencies, or whatever else it's buying.

An increase in the price of a bond translates to a decrease in the interest rate paid by the bond. It's easy to see why. A bond is just a piece of paper that promises the owner a certain amount of money in the future—say $100 next year. If the price of this bond is $97 today, then the bond is paying an interest rate of 3% because the $100 the bond pays out next year is 3% more than the $97 an investor pays for it today. Now if the price of the bond increases to $98, the interest rate paid by the bond drops to 2%, because the $100 the bond pays out next year is only 2% more than the $98 an investor pays for it today. So when the central bank says it's going to decrease interest rates, it's saying that it's going to increase the number of dollar bills in the economy by buying our bonds and paying us in dollars.

Conversely, when the central bank wants to reduce the amount of money in the economy, it sells the bonds and gold and whatever else back to us, taking away our dollar bills as payment. This selling spree pushes down the price of bonds, meaning interest rates rise. So when the central bank announces that it's going to increase interest rates, it's saying that it will reduce the number of dollar bills in the economy by selling us bonds and taking our dollars away.

Besides controlling the money supply, the central bank helps maintain the stability of the banking system. Remember that our fractional reserve banking system is especially susceptible to failure. Even a healthy bank will fail if people lose confidence and withdraw their deposits or otherwise refuse to trade with it. The central bank increases the stability of the banking system by standing ready to lend to banks whenever they need a temporary infusion of cash. It can credibly perform this function because the central bank itself will never run out of money. It can always just print more.

# CHAPTER 21

# Unemployment

Sometimes people can't find work, even when they are earnestly looking for it. These are not people who decide not to work because they won the lottery, or saved up enough to retire, or prefer to make do with welfare checks, or are disabled. These are people who want to work at jobs for which they are qualified, are not asking for more than the prevailing wage, but have not yet found a job. These people are said to be unemployed.

Unemployment is puzzling. A person's labor is a useful resource. A well-functioning economy would use all of the economy's resources—all of its labor and capital—to produce useful things. In a free market system, if there are too many people seeking too few jobs, then wages should fall until it becomes attractive to hire everyone who wants a job. Just like if there's too much broccoli sitting around, its price will fall until it's snapped up. So why isn't this labor being snapped up? Why isn't this engineer building a bridge somewhere? Why isn't this nurse taking someone's temperature? Has the economy malfunctioned?

Maybe, but not necessarily.

Even in a well-functioning economy, there is bound to be some unemployment. It takes time for the right workers and the right firms to find each other. Just like it takes time for people to find the right spouse. This explains why unemployment exists alongside job vacancies. Firms are looking for the right workers, and workers are looking for the right firms. It can take a while to go through job postings and resumes, schedule interviews, and decide on the best fit. During this time, the worker is unemployed. This type of unemployment is known as *frictional unemployment*. It is unavoidable and does not imply a malfunctioning economy.

But often, unemployment is caused by deeper structural problems in the system. For example, minimum wage laws create unemployment by blocking firms from hiring low-skilled employees. If Abby can knit a sweater in an hour, and sweaters sell for $10, then Abby's output is $10 per hour. If there's a law that requires that Abby be paid at least $20 an hour, no one will hire Abby. She will remain permanently unemployed.

A minimum wage law is just one of many ways in which the labor market can get jammed. Other common culprits: The law mandates excessively high benefits. Or it may be illegal to fire someone once they are hired, making firms hesitant to hire in the first place. Unions, which are essentially cartels of workers, are another problem. Just as cartels of firms can collude to raise the price of what they are selling, cartels of workers can collude to raise the price of what they are selling—their labor. The above-market wages negotiated by unions using the threat of strikes prevent firms from hiring as many workers as they otherwise would have. Union workers gain at the expense of the firm's owners, its customers, and the non-union workers who can't get a job and become permanently unemployed.

Such structural dysfunctions are major sources of unemployment in many countries. The problem is easily solved by letting labor markets operate freely. But that can only happen once voters understand basic economics and support its simple prescriptions.

The frictions and structural forces described in this chapter create a baseline level of unemployment in the economy during normal times. Recessions, which are somewhat mysterious periods of falling output, will usually cause unemployment levels to rise above this baseline. We will talk about recessions in the next chapter.

# CHAPTER 22

# Recessions

Economies usually grow over time. Every year, we grow more pineapples and catch more fish than the year before. There are two reasons for this. First, technology improves. People figure out how to do more with the same resources. We grow more pineapples on the same patch of land after discovering fertilization. Second, because the economy saves and invests a portion of its output, there is more capital this year than there was the year before—we have more roads, factories, and airplanes that we can now use. These extra resources translate to extra output.

But this long-term upward trajectory is occasionally interrupted by periods of decline where the economy produces less than it did before. These aberrant periods of falling output are called *recessions*. Sometimes they last only a year or two. Sometimes they last a decade or more.

Economists agree about most things, but not on the causes and cures for recessions. We just don't understand the phenomenon all that well. There are plenty of conjectures and hypotheses and informed opinions. But unlike with the issue of free markets versus central planning, history hasn't given us a neat experiment to clarify recessions. I'll go ahead and outline some scenarios that illustrate the forces that might be at work. But keep in mind that these are all just possibilities to further explore. Nothing's really settled.

Sometimes, the reason for a recession may be straightforward: a drought destroys the crops or a plague ravages the population. Political instability and civil war put Liberia in a recession for much of the 1980s and 1990s. The global financial crisis of 2008 disrupted the flow of capital and set off recessions in many countries. These recessions had obvious proximate causes.

But often, the reasons for a recession are less clear. And even if a recession begins with an obvious event like a drought or a banking crisis, it might unleash other subtler forces that prolong the problem or increase its severity. To illustrate some of these subtler forces that might be at work, let's go back to our old friend Max on his island.

For many years now, Max has been growing and eating pineapples. One day he tires of eating pineapples and decides he'd like plums instead. So he figures out how to grow plums, clears his pineapple field, plants plum trees, waits for the plum trees to grow, discovers there's a beetle on the island that's eating the plums, invents a pesticide to eradicate the beetles, sprays the pesticide, finds out the pesticide gives him skin rashes, invents a new pesticide, sprays the new pesticide, and finally, many years after embarking on the project, he gets his first full harvest of plums. During this transition from pineapples to plums, Max wasn't producing much of either pineapples or plums. So Max's island economy was in a recession. This recession didn't imply any sort of error. It simply was a necessary consequence of change.

Our economies experience this type of change all the time. Tractors replace horse-drawn plows. E-mails replace handwritten letters. It seems plausible that particularly large shocks that necessitate a lot of restructuring will create recessions. For example, a lot of houses got built in the United States during a housing boom that lasted from 2000 to 2006. After house prices began to fall, it seemed that too many houses had been built too soon, and that the engorged housing sector should shrink. Moving construction workers and real estate agents into other jobs in other sectors takes time. They will be unemployed while things get sorted out. It seems likely that the necessary shift from housing to other sectors contributed to the powerful recession that gripped the country after the housing boom ended.

Recessions may also be caused by a general lack of confidence. If Max worries that unicorns will eat his pineapples, he won't plant pineapples. Even if the unicorns aren't real, the pineapples are gone. Confidence is particularly important when people are highly interdependent on each other, as they are in modern economies. Since we don't produce everything we need and instead rely on trading with others, we might worry about what those others are up to. What if they won't buy our pineapples in the fall? Should we scale back and plant less this year? Concerns about the economy can damage the economy, much like concerns about a bank failure can cause a bank to fail.

But these are all just conjectures. Nobody knows for sure why a large, complex, interconnected group of people ended up producing less this year than they did the year before. Since the cause is uncertain, the remedies are controversial. There is much disagreement about what the government can do, if anything, to ease recessions and get the economy going again.

If a recession is caused by droughts or plagues or reorganizations, there is nothing the government can or should do. The economy is working precisely as it should. It's just that you can't grow as many pineapples when there's a drought or a plague or a reorganization. If, on the other hand, the recession is caused by a civil war, then, obviously, ending the civil war will help. If it's caused by a financial crisis, then ending the financial crisis will help.

But what if it's lack of confidence that's holding people back? Here, the potential remedies get more controversial. One possibility is for the government to print up lots of dollar bills and mail them to everyone. This will eventually cause all prices to rise, causing no real change in people's wealth. But before prices catch up, maybe people will feel rich and start buying things from each other, getting things going again. This strategy, which essentially tries to trick people into behaving normally again, is called a *monetary stimulus*.

The government could go even further and spend money directly, snapping people out of their pessimism that no one is ever going to buy what they make. This is called a *fiscal stimulus*. But a massive spending spree by the government runs the risk of wasting the economy's resources in useless projects. Can the government spend wisely enough, given that the economy is incredibly complicated and government officials have little incentive to get things right? Can we prevent politically-connected contractors and other interest groups from hijacking spending decisions? Will the wastage be small enough and the benefits large enough to justify this course of action? Reasonable people can disagree on this.

The lean and uncertain years of a recession are, no doubt, painful. And unfortunately, we don't know enough about how to fix the problem. But we must also keep recessions in perspective. The United States enjoys greater prosperity than Bangladesh not because it managed its recessions better, but because it structured its economy better. It's easier to start a business in the United States. It's easier to hire and fire workers as needed. It's easier to get a good education. It's easier to access courts when a contract is not honored. These structural differences—the topics of the other chapters in this book—are the more important determinants of an economy's well-being.

# CHAPTER 23

# Public Goods

Markets do a great job of running the economy—they pull together the right resources to produce the right things and get them to the right people. But no system is perfect, and the market is no exception.

Markets stumble when it comes to a special type of good called a *public good*. What's special about a public good is that it's jointly consumed by a group of people. It cannot be divided up between them. Everyone in the group has to consume the exact same thing. Moreover, no one can be prevented from consuming the good, whether or not they've paid for it. As you can imagine, this makes for a pretty crazy situation, ripe for dysfunction. And dysfunction we get.

Let's say we want to install streetlights downtown. Everyone loves the idea—it'll make downtown safer and nicer for them. The city has one million residents, each willing to pay $20 for a safer and nicer downtown. So, all together, the streetlights generate a value of $20 million to the city's residents. They cost only $10 million, so they clearly should be installed.

But how? You could try to raise the money needed by persuading everyone to contribute $10 each. After all, they value the streetlights at $20, so it should be easy to get them to part with just $10, right? No, because even if a person refuses to pay, once the streetlights are installed, there's no way to stop that person from enjoying the benefits. So no one contributes, knowing that their personal contribution won't determine whether or not they get the benefits. So no money gets raised. And no streetlight gets installed. What was rational for the individual was irrational for the group.

Unfortunately, many of the things we want are public goods. A simple example is the military. If we live in the same country, we must share a military force that can protect us from foreign invasions. It's not like I can get my own military and you can get yours. And once we have a military, I can't be excluded from enjoying its protection even if I didn't pay for it. It's not like the military can selectively protect you from an invasion and not me. So I can't be persuaded to voluntarily pay for a military even though I value it.

There are many other examples of public goods: fountains in the town square, clean air, fixing the ozone layer, population control, world peace, and discovering the laws of physics. These are all important things that I value a lot. I'd be willing to pay thousands of dollars for them. But I'll get exactly the same thing whether I pay for it or not. So I won't pay for it. And neither will you. And neither will anyone else. So we don't get enough of these goods. We end up with too few fountains and physicists and too much pollution and wars and population growth.

Let's do a simple back-of-the-envelope calculation. Pick one of the above goods and think about how much you're willing to pay for it. If just 10% of the world values it as much as you do, how much would everyone together be willing to pay for it?

I'll go first: I'm willing to spend $5,000 to fix the ozone layer. If 10% of the world's population is like me, there are 700 million people willing to pay that much for this good. If we all ponied up, it would raise $3.5 trillion! In other words, fixing the ozone layer is a very valuable good worth $3.5 trillion to society. It's probably obtainable for much less than that—by hiring scientists to figure out new ozone-friendly techniques, retrofitting existing factories, hiring lawyers to sue firms that are illegally polluting, paying firms to cut their emissions if they are legally allowed to pollute, and so on. But it's not going to happen. Because whether or not I personally pay won't determine whether or not I get my ozone layer fixed. So I don't pay. Nobody pays. And we're stuck with a hole in the sky.

The solution to the problem of public goods is to enlist the political process. I won't voluntarily pay $10 for installing streetlights downtown. But I will still vote to forcibly collect $10 from everyone, including me, to pay for it. In other words, we can use the strong arm of the government to raise money from all of us through compulsory taxes and spend it on the appropriate public goods.

While this may be the best solution, we must also not forget the dangers. Remember that central calculations are virtually impossible to get right. How can the government know that installing streetlights is worth $20 million? How can it know that fixing the ozone layer is worth $3.5 trillion? Surveys and referendums can help reduce, but not nearly eliminate, the errors. Moreover, politics and lobbying—and not pure economic rationale—will influence which projects get funded and which contractors get used. Even so, the benefits of obtaining the most important public goods will outweigh the costs of using an imperfect government to procure it. I personally feel that the government should be involved in reducing pollution, containing population growth, and funding basic scientific research. My gut feeling is that the cost of procuring these shared goods is less than what all of us together are willing to pay for them. So that's how I would vote. But I could be wrong. What do you think?

We, as a society, have to decide many important questions like these. To decide well, ordinary people like you and me need to know a little economics. Unfortunately, most people don't know any. It's easy to see why: knowledge of economics is a public good. If everyone learned economics, we would vote for better policies that would give us all a better life. But your personally learning economics won't make the slightest difference, because your one vote won't affect anything. You get the same system whether you learn economics or not. So you don't learn ec—wait a second. You did learn economics! How wonderful! Now you just have to go out and teach everyone else. Good luck!

# What Next?

Congratulations on finishing a whole entire book on economics. It was short, but you've learned a lot. Reward yourself with a pat on the back and your favorite cookie. What the heck—make it two pats and two cookies. You deserve it. I mean, you actually finished a book on economics. Wow!

But don't hang up just yet. Visit my website for videos, book recommendations, and other fun and useful stuff. You can also subscribe to my mailing list to be notified when I release more books (my next one will be on personal finance). Head on over to

benmatheweconomics.com

And if you liked this book, tell people you know. Maybe they'll learn economics too. And they'll tell the people they know. Soon everyone will know economics and we'll be living in a supereconomy. Make it happen!

Made in the USA
Lexington, KY
29 July 2014